RANDY
AND
ME
AND OTHER STORIES

TOM MANCHESTER

ISBN: 979-8-89175-045-6 (sc)
ISBN: 979-8-89175-046-3 (ebk)

PROLOGUE

I've been telling my wife these stories for 28 years or so, and she would laugh. But, eventually, she would tell me: "This is the 20th time you've told this story, and it's a good story, but I know how it ends."

When I retired it occurred to me that I should write them down, because they are good stories, and I should tell them to more people than just my wife.

This really is just a collection of stories, not a biography of either of us. I've tried to put things in chronological order, and Randy's little brother, Shawn, helped me with some of the details. But there are time gaps when we didn't see a lot of each other. The point of the exercise is just enjoying fun stories about the good and not-so-good times that I experienced with this extraordinary person: Randy Renfrow.

If you followed AMA professional racing in the 1980s and 90s, then you have certainly heard of him. If you did not (or perhaps you weren't born yet), then have fun learning about him through our adventures together.

– Tom Manchester

CONTENTS

Prologue..3

Chapter 1 7

Chapter 2 12

Chapter 3 15

Chapter 4 22

Chapter 5 24

Chapter 6 27

Chapter 7 30

Chapter 8 34

Chapter 9: 1987 45

Chapter 10 51

Chapter 11: 1990 54

Chapter 12: 1991 58

Chapter 13: 1992 60

Chapter 14: 1994 66

Epilogue 69

Yamaha RD350 78

Slot Car Racing 91

CHAPTER I

I met Randy Renfrow at House of Kawasaki in Triangle, VA, where I worked as a line mechanic after working the summer at a speed shop in Annapolis, MD, that didn't have enough business to keep me on. I was road racing a Yamaha RD350 on a pretty tight budget at the time. Randy was also a line mechanic, and he and Jay Duvon, who was shop foreman, both had AMA Professional Motocross licenses, and raced their Maicos most weekends. I worked my way into the routine of the shop and got to know everybody. Monday mornings were all about how racing had gone that weekend (except in the winter). And when you needed to put the engine back into a Z1 (very heavy), everybody helped out. When the junior guy was trying to push start an old BSA with leaking carburetors and it burst into flame, Randy was the first one on the job with the fire extinguisher.

One of the ways you know that you have been accepted into the hierarchy of a new job is when they start to mess with you (at least with guys). We all had cans of spray chemicals on our workbenches that were used for cleaning a n d lubrication. Contact cleaner was used for a lot of things, most importantly for cleaning ignition breaker points (anybody remember those?). Our Parts Department bought contact cleaner, brake cleaner, and chain lube from the same distributor, who gave us a discount. They were in the same sort of can, but with different labels. Randy figured out that those labels could be removed, using brake cleaner, which was a pretty powerful solvent, and then re-applied on a different can if you were tediously careful. Thus, one day, having installed and gapped new points on a Z1, I then tried to clean them with what looked to be contact cleaner, and sprayed a big glob of sticky chain lube all over them! It was a huge mess that took a while to clean up. I looked at the can, and the other chemical cans on my workbench and figured out what had happened. I didn't say anything, but that evening, I switched my chemical cans with the mechanic next to me after he had gone home. Interestingly, he didn't say anything either, and those cans worked their way around the shop until they finally ended up back on Randy's workbench!

Chain lube is a really sticky grease that is designed to penetrate and adhere to a motorcycle drive chain while it is going around the sprockets at pretty high speed. Any normal lubricant would be flung off very quickly. This persistently sticky property also made it useful for various shenanigans in the shop. One particularly insidious trick was to spray a fine bead of chain lube onto the top of a car's windshield wipers. It would adhere and go unnoticed until the next rain. When those windshield wipers were used on a wet windshield, it created a visual effect of iridescent rainbows that made it pretty hard to see and was very difficult to clean up. Not very nice, really.

You could also jam the nozzle, so it was stuck open, then put the can in the drawer of somebody's toolbox. Again, it made a huge mess that took a long time to clean up. Also not very nice.

We all worked on our race bikes after hours, and there was generally beer involved. I would put the empty beer cans on the wall between Randy's stall and mine. When he found them there in the morning, it pissed him off, and he would put a trash can at the end of the wall and sweep them into the trash can with his arm. When I learned of this, the logical thing would have been to apologize and stop leaving beer cans on the wall, which I eventually did. But for one last time, I left a few beer cans on the wall, and I put a wood screw through the bottom of one of them and screwed it into the wall. Since the screw was inside the can, he couldn't see that it was screwed in place. Of course, in the morning he did his usual sweep of the beer cans, but the one can wouldn't move, which caused him to whack it several times before he figured out what was going on.

Then there was Bannister, the sales manager. He liked to hang out in the shop with us mechanics and try to be one of the guys. His full name was Bannister Allen, and it irritated him that his customers would assume that he was just saying his last name first, and they would always call him Allen, or, worse still, Al. He came back from a dealer meeting with a name tag that clearly stated "Bannister Allen," and he started wearing it religiously. But one day he took it off long enough to go to lunch. Randy found it on Bannister's desk, slipped the card out of the holder and inserted a comma, so it now read "Bannister, Allen." He slipped it back into the holder. We found the name tag in the trash later that day.

Then there was Bannister's old Toyota. It was a pretty good old car, but the clutch was starting to slip. One morning, he proudly announced to us guys in the shop that he was finally getting his clutch fixed, and he would be leaving early that afternoon for his appointment. Mistake! We thought about what we could do, and Randy had the idea of slipping a small floor jack under the rear suspension and jacking the wheel, so it was barely off the ground, with the jack hidden by the wheel. Being a little guy, Randy was the obvious man for the job. I went up front and chatted up Bannister to keep him occupied. It worked perfectly. We, of course, were all watching from around the corner as Bannister got into the car to leave for his appointment. He started the car, put it in gear and let out the clutch, and the car went nowhere. Of course, the wheel that was jacked up was spinning, but he couldn't see that, and the symptom was exactly like a hopelessly worn-out clutch. He got out of the car, scratched his head and looked around, but the jack was completely hidden behind the wheel. He thought maybe bouncing the rear suspension might help, which he did, then tried to drive away again, to no avail.

That's when he decided that he needed our help, and walked around to the rear shop door. His face was red, and he discovered

9

us peaking around the corner and laughing. His face got even redder (Bannister's face could get pretty red), but he still didn't quite understand what was going on, and wanted us to give him a push, thinking the clutch might work enough to get him going if the car was moving already.

We walked out to car, and Randy, on the pretense that he was inspecting the car, crawled underneath and pulled out the jack and said, "Maybe this is the problem?"

Bannister's face achieved a new record for redness as he slowly went from confused to pissed-off, to realizing that he was going to be late if he didn't get going right away.

Both Randy and Jay were excellent motocrossers, and when they were racing locally and I was not racing that weekend, I went to see them. Randy was particularly skilled at starts, which are important in all forms of racing, but especially in motocross where you line up 40 abreast and funnel into a turn that can accommodate about three bikes at once. In those days, motocross tracks used backward falling gates for starts. The gate was about 18" high and leaned slightly backwards, toward the bikes. You were supposed to line up with your front wheel just enough behind the gate, so there was room for it to fall down in front of your bike when the starter released it. That way, if you jumped the start, you would just hold the gate in the up position and you couldn't go anywhere until you backed up and let it fall. Each rider had his own gate, so if one guy jumps the start, it doesn't hold up anyone else. The starter would show signs for three minutes, two minutes, and one minute. When they turned the one-minute sign sideways, that meant that the gate would fall anywhere from immediately to about five seconds after. We got a picture of Randy's bike with his gate still fully up, but with his front wheel doing a wheelie that cleared the gate. The gate had fallen by the time his rear wheel got to it, and he made it to the first turn four bike lengths ahead of anyone else. Technically, this was illegal, but no one could prove that he had actually jumped the start. He won that race, BTW.

Randy was fast, but he was not a big guy, and motocross is very tough on your body. Randy had his share of injuries, including a couple of broken collarbones, torn meniscus, and eventually a torn anterior cruciate ligament. We gave him an award plaque called "The Order of the Broken Crutch" to commemorate the fact that he was limping around all the time.

CHAPTER 2

By now, I was racing a Yamaha TZ250, a real, purpose-built race bike, in WERA races, with some success. On Monday mornings, I would cruise into work with a couple of trophies, looking fresh as a daisy, bike all clean and very sleek looking, while Randy's Maico was covered in mud, and he would be hurting from an injury or just plain physical abuse. His knees were getting to the point where motocross was not looking like a long-term possibility for him. We started talking about roadracing, and I pointed out that being a little guy was a real advantage in roadracing. Light weight meant better acceleration, and small size meant less wind resistance. We hatched a plan for him to try it out.

WERA* (Western-Eastern Roadracing Association) had a class for 650cc production bikes, and, at the time, the best bike for the class was the Kawasaki 650 4-cylinder. We happened to have two of them in the shop awaiting estimates for crash repair. One had mostly cosmetic damage from a low-side crash. The other was far more serious, the bike having run into a car. The front forks and swingarm were bent as were the handlebars, foot pegs, and various brackets. We surreptitiously swapped some of the damaged parts from the low-side bike to the bent bike, so it would be estimated as a total loss. Randy then bought it from the insurance adjuster for $300 on a salvage title.

Then we got to work. I straightened the forks, having some expertise at that skill. We rigged up a fixture on the hydraulic press so we could straighten the swingarm. The acetylene torch and some bending and hammering got all the other bent things straightened out. Randy actually spent some money for new racing-style handlebars and a pair of Koni shock absorbers. A quick engine tune-up and his race bike was ready! He had leather motocross pants that he could wear, and I loaned him an old leather jacket of mine.

We went to a WERA event at Summit Point West Virginia shortly thereafter, and I introduced Randy around and helped him through a couple practice sessions. It quickly became clear that he wasn't going to need a lot of my help as he started going pretty fast right away. Because he was a first-time novice, he had to wear an "X" on his back, so the more experienced riders would know to look out for him! He managed to qualify on the front row for his race. I was racing in Grand Prix class, which ran later in the day, so I was free to watch Randy's race. I gathered up some of my friends and dragged them to the starting line to watch one of Randy's famous starts.

The starting procedure was a lot like motocross, with the three-, two-, and one-minute signs, then the one-minute sign goes sideways and, usually very quickly, a flagman would wave the green flag to signal the start. They were respectful of people's clutches and rarely held the field very long after the one-minute sign went sideways. You were gridded five-abreast, with however many rows it took to accommodate the class.

Randy was on the outside of the front row, which was a good position from which to see the starter. And he had been watching and studying his mannerisms, so he knew by his movements when he was going to wave the flag. Randy had his right hand around the throttle, but his right forefinger on the front brake. At the one-minute sign it was clutch in and shift into gear. When the one-minute sign went sideways he let out the clutch and lit up the rear wheel, spinning and smoking spectacularly but with the front brake still on. When the flagman starting moving his right elbow, which always immediately preceded the flag, he released the front brake and rocketed away, front wheel about a foot in the air. He had about five bike lengths on the nearest competitor! He went on the win his very first roadrace!

*WERA started out as the East-Coast Roadracing Association – ERA. We had ERA bumper stickers, which would commonly be confused as having to do with the Equal Rights Amendment, a big issue in the day. Eventually, the ERA started promoting races all over the country, including California, so they changed the name to Western-Eastern Roadracing Association, which sounds a little goofy, but everyone just says the acronym: WERA.

CHAPTER 3

The shop where we both worked closed later that summer. I took a job at a motorcycle mechanics' training school in College Park, MD, while Randy bought a dump truck. But we still saw each other at Summit Point when there was a WERA race. I would be fussing over my bike, jetting the carburetors, peering at the spark plugs, worrying over what slick tires to run and getting the tire pressures just right. Randy would sit in a lawn chair in his swim trunks. The only prep he did was to put gas in it. And it being a 4-stroke, it was just straight gas, unlike my bike which needed gas mixed with oil in a very precise ratio. And he was getting a reputation for being really fast. He had a friend and fan from Fredericksburg, VA (where Randy lived), named Doc Bigoney, who loaned him a Honda CB750F to race. Doc was a podiatrist and a motorcycle rider with several bikes. He was too old to race himself, so he raced vicariously via Randy. The CB750F was a pretty good race bike. Randy would race the Kawasaki in 650cc Production class and 650cc Superbike (modified production) class. He raced the Honda in 750cc Production and Superbike classes. The Honda's only shortcoming was its transmission, and when it failed, Randy would run the Kawasaki in all four classes, generally winning all four races! He went on to win four

WERA National Championships that year, mostly riding the salvaged ($300) Kawasaki 650!

In the meantime, I got an AMA (American Motorcyclist Association, nothing to do with doctors) Professional Roadrace license and raced my TZ250 at Daytona, with some success. I bought a brand new 1980 TZ250G for the next year and raced it at Daytona, then at Charlotte Motor Speedway. I had done some tuning on it after Daytona, and it was a rocketship at Charlotte, except that I had a bad crash, breaking my left radius, my left tibia, and my right thumb. I also bent the bike up pretty well. This put me out of commission for a few months. I passed the time doing telephone sales for Time-Life books. Don't hate me! We only called people who had already responded to a mailer, the books were good, and we would always hang up after three unanswered rings. When you're recovering from broken bones, you aren't sick, so you can get pretty bored. Selling books gave me something productive that I could do with a cast on my leg and casts on both arms!

There were a lot of small motorcycle dealers around the Washington D.C. area, but the big ones were Hersons in Maryland, Cycles Incorporated in Arlington, VA, and Cycle Sport Unlimited in Tysons Corner, VA. Cycle Sport was not as big as the other two, but had a dedicated following thanks to their focus on the recreational use of motorcycles. The owner, Dave Nees, was a motocross racer, and then a nationally ranked professional roadracer. His business model was to sell fun bikes for all sorts of activities, on and off road, and then provide activities and venues for his customers and potential customers to enjoy their motorcycles. Cycle Sport was a Yamaha dealer, but also sold Maicos and a few other very small volume brands.

Dave Nees was a tall, lanky guy. When he was roadracing, he was known as "Dave Knees and Elbows" because he had difficulty fitting his long, skinny frame behind the fairing. So his knees, elbows, and feet were always sticking out. Dave was a dedicated motorcycle sportsman, but he was also a good businessman. When a small

Yamaha shop in Springfield, VA, (the other side of the Capital Beltway in Virginia) came up for sale, he bought it.

He hired Randy Renfrow to be General Manager, and sent Beth Wriska from the Tysons Corner store to run the Parts Department. Randy was getting tired of driving his dump truck and getting up at 4:30AM every morning. He liked the idea of being able to implement all the ideas he had from working in various motorcycle shops. He also had a good head for business, a strong customer focus, and a concept that service should drive sales, rather than the other way around.

Beth was 19 years old, cute and blond! She really knew Yamaha parts, and the customers quickly learned to respect her. That summer, I got the casts off of my arms and was able to do manipulative skills again, though I was till dragging around a pretty big cast on my left leg. The Time-Life Books thing was fine when that was all I could do, but now that I could do real work again, it got to be pretty boring. I had heard about the new Cycle Sport-Springfield store and called Randy about working there. The hiring had to go through the Tysons Corner office. I was hired as a mechanic to begin with, but with the understanding that John Boucher, the long-time Service Manager, planned to leave mid-summer and that I would take over as Service Manager.

This shop was in a strip mall and was originally a tile store. It had a front space that was a showroom, big enough for tile displays, but pretty small for motorcycles, and a warehouse area behind, that was barely big enough for three motorcycle lifts. It had been run as a "mom & pop" motorcycle business for the past 12 years, selling less than 100 units per year. It never once turned a profit during those 12 years. The back door out of the shop opened onto a loading dock, and there was a wooden ramp that allowed us to push bikes in and out of the shop to the parking lot behind. The problem was that the door was just not quite wide enough for a bigger bike's handlebars, so you had to master the technique of turning the bars slightly sideways in order to fit through the door, then straightening them again once you got through. All of this while maintaining enough momentum to get up the ramp.

Since the shop was so small, we had to push all the bikes out into the back parking lot in the morning in order to have any room for doing work. We ran a chain through their wheels and locked them up for security during the day. Then at night we had to push them all back into the shop. At that point in the day, we were tired, and we were pushing them up the ramp, not down. However, everybody in the store pitched in, and it became a team-building exercise before any management gurus thought of that concept.

We'd screw around with each other. If you were next to the ramp and somebody was halfway up, furiously pushing a bike, you could grab a foot peg or something to slow them down, which put them into a very wobbly situation. Of course, you would then help them get going again. You didn't want a customer's bike to fall over, especially on top of you! The biggest, heaviest bike Yamaha sold at the time was based on the 4-cylinder XS1100 (we called it the "EXcessive 1100") that was then festooned out with a big front fairing, trunk, and saddlebags. We called that version the "Battlestar." It weighed in at over 800 pounds, and its brakes had a tendency to drag, making it a challenge to push up that ramp. However, we had a young guy named TJ working for us who was as strong as a horse. TJ was pushing a "Battlestar" up the ramp when Randy decided to mess with him and grab the rail on the back of the trunk as TJ was halfway up. Instead of messing up TJ, it pulled Randy off of his feet, and TJ never even noticed!

That summer and fall we focused on getting service work done efficiently, and following up with our service customers. They would call it Client Relationship Management in modern business-speak, but we just saw it as good business, and we didn't have any software to help.

Come winter, it was just down to Randy, Beth, and I. We sold some minibikes as Christmas gifts. I still had a small cast on my leg when I was delivering a minibike to an anxious mom. I saw her looking nervously at my cast, and I quickly explained that it was from a skiing accident, not to worry!

We also had a trickle of service work, and I sent out mailers to our service customers advertising winter storage with discounted service pricing during the storage period. It snows in Virginia in the winter, and a lot of people just throw a cover over the bike and hope that it fires up in the spring without too much difficulty. This leads to ruined batteries, flat tires, clogged carburetors, rusted gas tanks…all sorts of problems that need to be sorted out before you can ride when the weather turns nice. We took care of all that stuff so their bike was clean, tuned-up and ready to go in the spring. We also painted the shop, set up a proper shop ventilation system, and replaced the old motorcycle lifts.

Mostly, we were getting ready for next year. Yamaha had a plan to take over Honda as the largest motorcycle brand in the United States. That plan involved several new models with attractive pricing and a big increase in production. Through our parent store, it was decided that Cycle Sport-Springfield would sell 400 motorcycles the next year! …from a storefront that had never reached 100 sales in one year.

We planned…we could only have three mechanics and one helper, because that's all we had the physical space for, so we needed really good guys, and we needed to work the hell out of them. That meant we had to pay them really well and treat them really well. We also had to be ready. When you are in service, your biggest problem is always parts. When a bike is waiting on parts, it is taking up space and wasting precious time for you and your customer. Beth, Randy, and I mapped out what we were going to sell, month-by-month, then mapped out when those bikes would be in for service, and pro-jected a month-by-month parts order that would give us exactly the parts we needed, when we needed them.

Come January, the business office in Tysons Corner informed us that Cycle Sport-Springfield had earned a net profit of $5,000 for CY1980! This was the first time that shop had ever earned a profit!

Sometime during that winter, it became clear to me that there was something going on between Beth and Randy. Beth was always dolled up, but she seemed to be more so, and Randy seemed to know a lot about her mom and her sister. Beth kept using the pronoun "we" a lot when speaking of her and Randy. When Beth would be arranging displays in the showroom and Randy would offer criticism, she would give him a look that said, "And do you think you will be getting any tonight?" Being employee and boss, this was not really a proper relationship in a business. I was told that Dave Nees was aware of it, and that he had told them that it could go on under the condition that they were completely discreet. So, I kept it to myself except when among the three of us.

We both stood up for Beth when macho customers didn't trust her expertise. She would be standing behind the parts counter, and a customer would ask her if he could speak to the Parts Manager. When she explained that she WAS the Parts Manager, they would ask for the Service Manager, so she would go and fetch me. The guy would ask for something like a throttle cable for a YZ250, and I would say, "I don't really know if we have that or not. You'll have to ask Beth." I'd call Beth back and ask her if she could help this gentleman (NOT) out.

When I was a kid, my brothers and I would amuse ourselves during a long car ride by looking at signs and spelling them backwards. For instance "Park" turned into "Krap," which we found very amusing as little kids. When I saw Randy's last name on the back of his leathers, I immediately saw that "Renfrow" became "Worfner." Beth found that to be amusing and started calling Randy by that name.

Randy was still doing WERA races, but he was beginning to have greater ambitions. When I brought my poor, wrecked TZ250G into the shop, he told me to go ahead and order all the parts I needed to repair it. His plan was to borrow it and get enough WERA points on it to qualify for an AMA Professional Roadrace license for 1981. We took it to a WERA race in Rockingham, NC, where he rode it in every class it was eligible to race, including the Open Grand Prix class for 750, 900, and 1000cc race bikes. He won everything but the open class (2nd place!) and garnered enough points for his AMA Pro license. He also rode a Yamaha 550 Seca 4-cylinder (from the shop) in the production classes, and beat the 650s and 750s on it.

Watching him, people would question whether the bike could possibly be stock, when he would out-accelerate much bigger bikes off the turns. I would show them the point in the turn at which Randy got on the gas, and how much later the other bike did. His bike didn't accelerate harder, it just started accelerating much sooner!

That winter Randy ordered a new Yamaha TZ250H. This was a pure race bike, but unlike previous versions where the engine was based on a street bike, the "H" model was a unique, new design, completely optimized for racing. It was a thing of beauty! And when it arrived in February, we set it up and took it out to Summit Point to shake it down. Confoundingly, it leaked oil, and with three professional mechanics on hand, we could not fix it or even identify the source. Back at the shop, I pulled the engine out and started looking at it closely. I realized that the sand-cast engine cases were porous, and the oil was seeping right through them when it got hot. By now, I was good friends with the technical people at Yamaha, so I called and explained the situation, and Randy's intent to campaign the bike in AMA professional competition. I managed to get them to agree to warranty the engine cases and all the other parts required to complete the repair. This on a bike that clearly says: "Sold as is. No warranty expressed or implied."

CHAPTER 4

When March arrived, we were ready at the shop. We had hired Billy Spelios as chief mechanic and shop foreman. Billy was a top-notch mechanic with a strong work-ethic and a passion for quality. Two other experienced mechanics and TJ as helper filled out the team. When the semi-truck arrived with 40 motorcycles in crates, they went onto the loading dock, and we had absolutely no place to store them. We had to get them all set up that night. My job was to bust down crates and get all the trash out of the way as quickly as possible. Randy flew for pizza and beer. Beth pushed the finished bikes into the showroom, the Parts Department, or wherever there was an open space. We got everything done about midnight. Our guys earned about three hours flat rate time for each bike, and we gave them 50 percent overtime pay, so they knew they were going to get a really big paycheck. We let them sleep in the next morning.

Randy had hired a full-time sales manager and another salesperson to move these bikes, which we did. We needed to, because that same delivery scenario would repeat itself another 10 times over the course of the spring and summer.

We sold 400 bikes that year out of our little shop, and we made more profit than the Tysons Corner store! And it was all about efficiency in the back and customer service in the front.

Trash Cans

There was a long-standing practice of using old 55-gallon oil drums for trash cans in auto and motorcycle shops. They are free, and they are perfectly suited for the job of holding heavy, dirty, oily stuff. You empty them into the dumpster and are done with that trash. The first motorcycle shop where I worked, in Chicago, the tradition was to make the new guy (me) empty the trash cans. We had a huge dumpster that was too tall to dump them straight in, so at the end of the day, we brought all the trash cans outside with the fork lift, then I had to ride up on the fork lift and dump them into the dumpster about six feet in the air. This is Chicago, so there is always a 30 mile per hour wind blowing, and I had to balance on the tines of the fork lift!

We had 55-gallon drums for trash cans at Cycle Sport, and we emptied them into the dumpster every night. Two guys could lift and dump them without big problems, no fork lift needed. In those days if you spilled oil on the floor, you soaked it up with kitty litter and threw it out in the trash can. Also, oil filters and empty oil bottles went in there. These days, there are strict EPA rules about dealing with oily stuff, but in those days, it all just went out with the trash.

Randy was a neatnik. Frankly, so am I, but I'm all about efficiency. One day, Randy told me he thought we should be using plastic liners in the trash cans, so they didn't get so dirty. I responded: "Randy…they're 55-gallon oil drums. They're dirty already. That's why we use them for trash cans!"

He explained that his mother cleaned the kitchen counters with 409 every night, whether she had cooked anything or not!

I said: "Your mother is a saint. She's put up with you all these years, hasn't she? We're not so saintly." We went back and forth about it, so I said: "If you can convince the guys in the shop that it's a good idea, then I'm okay with it." The guys in the shop immediately responded that they fill the cans with sharp, heavy, metal stuff, and that plastic liners would be torn and split right away, not practical at all. I won that argument!

CHAPTER 5

Randy started his professional roadracing career that spring at Pocono International Raceway. There was a very experienced guy named Bill Himmelsbach that we knew from WERA racing at Summit Point. Randy trailed Himmelsbach in 6th place for much of the race, then finally got by him toward the end. Once past, he caught up and passed the next guy to take 4th place in his first attempt. He raced several more pro races that year, culminating in a 2nd place at Daytona behind Jimmy Felice, a guy who was even smaller than Randy!

We had a nice party on Christmas Eve at Cycle Sport – Springfield that year. We invited clients and had some holiday cheer. Beth liked a drink called a Black Emerald. You fill a cordial glass half full of Tia Maria, then use the back of a spoon to float Baileys Irish Cream on top. You are supposed to toss it down as a shooter, but you miss all the flavor that way. One young guy got a little bit hammered and decided that he liked Beth. Officially, Beth and Randy were not supposed to be going together, so I became Beth's boyfriend for long enough to discourage Romeo!

We greatly expanded our winter storage and service program that year. We rented a big self-storage locker and kept on Billy and TJ. TJ shuttled bikes back and forth, and Billy did the services. One day, I needed TJ to run some errands, so I looked in the shop and asked, "TJ, what are you doing now?"

He replied immediately, "I'm charging batteries."

I thought about that for a second…you hook a battery up to a charger, and that's all there is to it. Then I said, "Well maybe those batteries can spare your attention long enough for you to run up to Tysons Corner and get some parts for Billy, so he can get some work done?!"

But I laughed to myself!

The next spring, we were able to hire two very good mechanics from a Kawasaki shop in Alexandria that had closed. One guy had been the service manager there – Norvin Stevens. Norvin was a good fellow and a very experienced mechanic, but it turned out that his wife had left him, and he was in the midst of a personal depression. Our shop was in a strip mall, and there was a bar/restaurant at the end of the strip called the Ranch House. We'd stop there for a drink once in while after a tough day. Norvin, however, would go there every day after work and would often close the place down, with little motivation to go home. Randy and I both knew that he should be a top performer at work, and that he wasn't doing it. But Randy jumped in to help in a way that would have been very difficult for me. He got Norvin into an AA program and kept on him to make sure it was working. He really got Norvin straightened out, and it was a good lesson in people management for me.

Randy believed in God. He wasn't religious per se, but he was very strong on the values that he was taught as a child. His father had been a Marine Gunnery Sergeant and his mother was active in their church. He never preached to anyone, but you could always tell that he was very grounded in his personal beliefs. He told me once that on the starting line at a race, before he put on his helmet and gloves, he would close his eyes for a moment and ask God to make him humble. Myself, I was always busy thinking about my tire pressures, chain adjustment, and that sort of thing. Humility was the last thing on my mind. It seemed to work for Randy.

1982 was an interesting year in our business. Yamaha was still aggressively pursuing Honda for #1 in sales, but the market was beginning to saturate. Norvin's store in Alexandria shut its own doors. But there was a shop just down the street from us in Springfield, VA, that was locked up by the sheriff. Most dealers, both car and motorcycle, buy their inventory on "floor plan," meaning they are financed by a bank, and that bank owns the title of each unit until it is sold at retail. At that point, the dealer has to pay off the bank in order to transfer title to the new owner. If the unit stays in inventory, you pay a monthly interest charge to the bank, so, as a dealer, you are motivated to get it sold. But unlike cars, motorcycles are delivered in crates that are covered in a big, cardboard box. This dealer was uncrating motorcycles very carefully and then reassembling the crate, so it looked undisturbed. You could stack that crate (using a forklift) on top of other, normal crates, so the VIN was visible to an inspector. Then you could sell the bike to a retail customer and have at least a month float before you had to pay the bank. This can help get a dealer through a tough month. It becomes a problem when you have multiple tough months, as this dealer had. It is known as "selling out of trust," and it is illegal. When customers who had bought their bikes in May had still not received their state license plates in July, they began to complain to the DMV, who investigated and found that the title had never been transferred. Thus the sheriff's intervention.

At Cycle Sport, we were doing pretty good with sales, but not making a lot of profit on it. Thankfully, we attracted service business from all over and that business easily covered our overhead. Randy came up with the slogan: "Cycle Sport-Springfield, the House that Service Built." He and I took a lot of pride in that. And we took a lot of pride that he, Beth, and I had made a thriving business out of what had been a tiny, hobby-shop operation.

CHAPTER 6

In the meantime, I had gotten married, bought a condominium in Washington D.C., and was thinking about the future. I had tried racing again and visited some of my bucket-list tracks (Watkins Glen, etc.), but the way my left leg was broken prevented me from getting my foot out of the way in left hand turns, so I was competing for 21st instead of first. Mind you, racing is dangerous, and it is expensive. If it is NOT FUN, then it's pretty stupid. So, my race bike went away, and I started thinking of a future that would be fulfilling in other ways. A position came open at Northern Virginia Community College (NOVA, which had a big automotive program), for a motorcycle and small engine instructor. I applied and got the job, starting that September. I had taught motorcycle mechanics before and liked it, and I liked the academic environment. I found out that I also liked to design training classes, because the course designs that I inherited were about 30 years old.

Norvin, a former service manager who was now on his feet and perfectly capable of taking my place, was made service manager at Cycle Sport at my recommendation. Things went well at NOVA, and I made friends there. We had an arrangement with General Motors that we could attend any of their classes at their Fairfax Training Center at no charge, and I took full advantage of that. I became known as the "cover whatever" guy. If one of the instructors/professors had to miss a class, I would attend the class as a student in the morning, then teach it that evening. They also sent me to Evinrude/Johnson school, as well as Bear Brakes and Alignment school. I was busy that winter. But most of my classes were night classes, and I had time to play golf (Norvin taught me to play golf), and I had time to keep in touch with Cycle Sport.

Yamaha's strategy to beat Honda was finally catching up with them, and they had drastically overproduced. They had unsold crates of very nice 4-cylinder motorcycles that had now been sitting for three years and had big problems. The carburetors were clogged, the gas tanks were rusted, and in some cases the brake master cylinder return ports were clogged, so the brakes would lock on every time you applied them. Cycle Sport could buy these bikes for almost nothing, and warranty would pay whatever it took to make them ready for sale. I had time during the day (night class guy) and was very familiar with these bikes. So, I made a deal with Randy and Norvin that I would come in once or twice a week and set up three bikes, assembly line style, clean the carburetors, clean the rust from the gas tanks, adjust the valves, set the idle mixtures on the exhaust gas analyzer, and make them perfect. I flagged nine hours labor on each bike, and I did it in time to get to my night class at NOVA...sweet!

But this was 1983, and Randy was getting serious about professional racing. He and Beth broke up, and he conscripted Ron Barrick, a mechanic at Cycle Sport – Tysons Corner, to be his full time mechanic. Randy, Ron and Doc Bigoney went to all the AMA National Races. A race engine needs to rebuilt pretty often, though, and he still only trusted me to rebuild his crankshafts.

A 2-stroke crankshaft has a tough life, especially in a racing bike. Its lubrication comes from oil mixed in with the gas, and it is expected to (in Randy's bike) to rev to 13,000 RPM on a fairly continuous basis. After each race weekend I needed to remove it, inspect and/or replace the bearings and connecting rods, and true it. "True it?" Yes, it is a built-up crank made from precision machined flywheels, a pressed in rod bearing pin and a connecting rod, and needle rod bearing. You take it apart and put it back together on a hydraulic press. There are various clearances that need to be just so, like the rod side clearance, but once assembled, you check it for runout with dial gauges on each of the main bearing lands. The factory specification is 0.02mm (for you metricophobes 0.025mm = 0.001"). You could pay rebuild shops $500 to give you a rebuild to this tolerance. I would get Randy's crankshafts so the runout was the width of the line on the dial gauge. That means less than 0.001mm, the minimum that the gauge is capable of measuring. Any crankshaft runout becomes a binding force as the crank rotates, and when you minimize it, the crank revs more freely, and all the engine power goes to accelerating the bike instead of overcoming friction.

At the end of the season, Randy was AMA 250 National Champion! I took some vicarious satisfaction, in that I had helped Randy get started in roadracing and helped a little with prepping the bike.

Randy's championship also lent some additional prestige to the Cycle Sport organization. Cycle Sport organized roadrace training sessions at Summit Point periodically during the summer for people who had purchased Sport Bikes or who were considering it. Randy became the lead instructor. Ron Barrick and I sometimes were the shepherds, riding behind the groups on the track and keeping things organized. It also got him noticed by Starfire Insurance Company, who wanted to get into the motorcycle insurance business. Randy got sponsorship money from them in return for painting his bike with their logo. Their colors were an orangey-red and yellow. Randy said they were the same as Maico colors (he still held some loyalty to Maico), and he bought leathers to match. As club racers, we always dreamed of having corporate sponsorship. But it was an impossible dream, and here was my buddy Randy with a company paying him to race!

CHAPTER 7

Randy's success also motivated him to aim higher in 1984, and he bought a used Honda RS500 from Mike Baldwin in order to compete in the premier AMA professional class. The formula was modeled after the top world championship class for 500cc pure race bikes. However, the AMA grandfathered in the Yamaha TZ750s that had dominated the class for a decade, and they allowed 750cc Superbikes, which were highly modified street bikes that also ran in their own class. The premier class was called Formula 1 (the 250cc class was now called Formula 2) The RS500 was far more sophisticated than any of the other bikes in the class, and if you wanted to win, it was the bike you needed. It was much lighter than the TZ750s and could change direction much more quickly. The engine configuration was a 2-stroke V3! The V-angle pointed forward, with two cylinders pointing upward at about a 45-degree angle and one cylinder pointing downward at a similar angle. This helped keep the center of gravity low, but made for a peculiar problem in that the oil that was mixed with the gas would settle into the cylinder head of the downward cylinder when the bike was not running. It would then tend to foul the spark plug on restart. So, when the bike came into the pits after practice, the first step was always to remove the lower fairing section (six dzus fasteners) and remove the down cylinder spark plug. Of course, you had to remember to put it back in before restarting!

The bike also had a transmission that could be removed from the side of the bike. This feature made for the ability to change transmission ratios quickly and easily, in between one practice session and the next. With most other bikes, you needed to remove the engine from the frame and disassemble it to change gear ratios, if in fact alternate ratios were even available. That made it an overnight proposition.

The season began at Daytona in March. It is known as Motorcycle Speed Week, because there is a whole week of practice and qualifying, with Wednesday devoted to amateur racers. The main events are run on Friday, Saturday, and Sunday, including a Supercross event on a track set up in the infield. The feature event is the Daytona 200 for Formula 1 bikes. The track uses most of the banked oval, going into the infield for seven turns before going back onto the banking, then a chicane jukes off the back straight, then back onto the banking leading into the front straight. Top speed around the oval is very important to a fast lap time.

Daytona preceded the world championship grand prix season, so guys like Kenny Roberts and Freddie Spencer would show up with their new grand prix bikes to shake them down before the European season began. There were major factory teams from Honda, Yamaha, and Kawasaki with big semi-truck rigs and swarms of mechanics in team uniforms. Honda had a truck that was there to support all Honda-mounted competitors, with parts and engineering information at the ready. Randy made good enough friends with them that he was able to get some updated cylinders for his RS500.

Northern Virginia Community College had a short Spring Break going on during that time, so I was able to get down to Daytona for Thursday, Friday and the weekend, before flying home Sunday night. Randy had already managed to reach 182 MPH on the front straight!

That's when I met Jim Allen, the Dunlop tire man.

Goodyear, Michelin, and Dunlop were all there with tires. A win at Daytona was pretty good advertising for them, and they competed to get the best riders on their tires. Randy had already worked with Dunlop in 1983 and knew Jim Allen as a friend. Jim was a great guy. He had obligations to the factory teams that Dunlop supported, but he would try to get Randy the special tires that were normally reserved for the factory teams. Jim recognized Randy's talent, but also his commitment and determination. He knew there was great potential there.

Most of the AMA races could be run on a single tank of gas, but not Daytona. Two-hundred miles would require two refueling stops using an overhead refueling rig that engaged a dry break valve in the gas tank. This required practice as you could lose precious seconds, both during refueling and during pit-in, pit-out riding. There were no pitlane speed limits then, so the rider headed toward a large pit board at very high speed, braking just in time to slightly nudge the pit board, while the mechanics got the nozzle pushed into the gas tank. A clear line on the side would show them when the tank was full, and their job was then to pull out the nozzle and get out of the way as quickly as possible. Two mechanics behind the bike would then push as the rider let out the clutch and took off.

Come race day we were pretty nervous, but excited. Randy had qualified well, but clearly behind the factory teams. As the race played out, Kenny Roberts took command with Freddie Spencer on a Honda behind. Eddie Lawson, Kenny's teammate had mechanical problems and dropped back. We did clean pit stops and kept Randy in the running. At the end, we were in 6th place, first non-factory entry, and ahead of several of the factory bikes. I had to hurry off to catch my plane home, but we were pretty happy with that effort, knowing that a lot of the guys who beat us were headed off to Europe and wouldn't be contesting the whole AMA series.

My summer got busy as I had applied for a job with American Honda Motor Co., Inc. as a district service manager based on an ad in Automotive News. I had three interviews, and it turned out that

I was being interviewed for a technical training instructor position. I eventually got the job and started on October 1, 1984. I trained in New Jersey, then took over my own training center in Windsor Locks, CT. I managed to get to a couple of Randy's races in 1985, but only as a spectator. The highlight was at Pocono, PA, where he finished a frustratingly close 2nd place to Mike Baldwin who was on a factory Honda, drafting down the straightaway and nearly getting by.

CHAPTER 8

In early 1986, Randy called me and told me that he had bought a brand-new Honda RS500, and that an Entrepreneur/Team Owner named Don Mclean had loaned him a Honda RS250 to compete in the 250 class. Randy wanted to know if I could come to the races and work on the 250 for him. I looked at my schedule and found that I could make a lot of the races, if not quite all of them, and I would usually have to fly in on Friday night, so I would miss Friday practice. We agreed to that arrangement.

1986 Brainerd, MN

I couldn't make it to Daytona, so my first event was the AMA National at Brainerd, MN, in northern Minnesota near the Canadian border. I had a training class to teach on Friday, so I caught an evening flight into Minneapolis. Randy had told me that the hotel where they were staying was only 15 minutes from the airport. I went to the Hertz office and asked for directions to Brainerd, and they said it was a four-hour drive! I told him what Randy told me, and he said he must be talking about the Brainerd Airport! I didn't even know there was a Brainerd Airport! In any case, it was 11:00 PM, and there were no flights there until tomorrow. So off I go in my rental with a stiff cup of coffee and a long drive ahead. I got to the hotel about 3:00 AM and tried to get a few hours' sleep before we headed out to the track.

I was sleepy that morning and screwed up immediately, trying to get the 250 into neutral, so I could push it to the pits for practice. It had been a while since I had dealt with a race bike, and I forgot that the shift pattern is opposite that of a street bike. So, I'm pushing the shift lever down and down, finally getting it into 6th gear and nowhere near neutral (between 1st and 2nd). I'm scratching my head, and Ron Barrick sees what I'm doing and reminds me to shift the lever up, not down. Feeling like a bonehead, I get it into neutral and find my way to the pits. There is a stand that engages the rear axle and levers the rear of the bike up. I figure this out, but nearly fall over while lifting it up!

Okay, I can do stuff like adjusting the chain, setting tire pressures, putting in gas. Randy runs a practice session, and the bike seems to be fast. Ron and I get the 500 ready for the next practice session. We have a big pitboard that w e use to tell Randy what his lap time was for the previous lap. He is competitive. His main rivals are Wayne Rainey riding for the Honda factory, and Kork Ballington, an Australian who had won 250 and 350 world championships before. He is riding for Don McLean. The announcer was Richard Chambers, an old friend from WERA racing, who had retired from racing himself a couple of years prior. As Richard announced lap times for the guys out practicing, Ron and I realized that he was not timing them himself, he was reading the times from the pitboards. So the next time around, we took five seconds off of Randy's lap time, and Richard announced it! Then he looked down at Ron and I who were waving at him, and he announced that we must be "joshing him!"

After practice, we debriefed and decided that the 250 would be quicker if we changed a couple of the gear ratios. This required the engine to come out and apart, so I started on that job while Ron and Doc Bigoney worked on the 500.

Minnesota is known as the Land of 1,000 Lakes, and it is particularly true in Northern Minnesota. When springtime arrives, those lakes turn into the perfect breeding grounds for mosquitos. The locals refer to the mosquito as the state bird and point out that only the really bad-ass mosquitos can survive there. The good news is that a mosquito can only survive a few seconds in direct sunlight. The men's room, however, is not in direct sunlight. Randy needed to use it after practice, and in his moment of vulnerability, a mosquito got him…yes…there, on his pecker! This resulted in subsequent embarrassing itching spells!

I was working away on the 250 transmission, and I had it ready for reassembly when I began to start swatting myself. I realized that the sun was setting, and the mosquitos were coming for me in swarms. Ron Barrick hollered to throw a tarp over the 250 engine, and that we would finish it in the morning. Then we got to the van, which had been left open with the dome light on. It was completely full of mosquitos! Randy found a new can of contact cleaner, which is mostly carbon tetrachloride, and will kill anything. He sprayed it into the van until it was empty, then told us to jump in and hold our breath until he got going. We got up some speed and stuck our heads out the windows to breathe until the van aired out enough to be safe.

I slept like a rock and felt great in the morning! We got to the track early, and I got the 250 all put back together in time for qualifying heats. There were some 250 specialists there who were fast, Donnie Green (three-time National Champion) and Rich Oliver, who had some podium finishes last year. Kork Ballington was also riding a 250 for this race, he being a former 250 World Champion! We qualified on the front row for both races and were feeling pretty good. The 250 race was right after lunch, and Randy got one of h i s patented holeshots and took the lead, followed closely by Kork Ballington. He continued to lead, but at the end Kork was closing and passed Randy on the last turn leading onto the straightaway and the finish line. Dang! When Randy came back into the pits, he showed me the clutch lever. The adjustment had come loose, and he could not disengage the clutch. He had ridden the last half dozen laps without being able to use the clutch to downshift. That caused him to run wide in the last turn and let Kork by. As the mechanic for the 250, I really should have checked and tightened the lock nut for the clutch adjustment, so it was my fault and I felt bad, though I hadn't realized that he had adjusted it before the race. Anyway, we got 2nd place and sprayed champagne all over everyone and everything. It made a sticky mess on the bike that was a pain to clean up.

Then came "The National," the feature race. I had to drive all the way back to Minneapolis to catch my flight, so I didn't get to watch it. But thankfully the local radio station was broadcasting it, and I listened in the car. Randy won—his first "National" win, beating Wayne Rainey, Kork Ballington, and a bunch of other very fast guys. He was on the podium wearing his Dunlop cap with the ESPN cameras on him.

I called him the next morning. He told me that he was, of course, completely focused during the race, but that afterward all he could think about was how much his mosquito bite itched, and here he was in front of TV cameras and interviewers. He had to tell himself: "NO...YOU CANNOT SCRATCH YOURSELF THERE!!"

Elkhart Lake, WI

Road America in Elkhart Lake, WI is one of the great race tracks in the world. It is 4.1 miles long and sits on the side of a fairly steep hill in the Wisconsin kettle moraine, the rocky terrain left by the receding glaciers from the last ice age. There is a long uphill straight that favors engine torque, so the TZ750s and Superbikes were more competitive here. There is also a steep downhill back straight that provides one of the Cojones Grandes moments of life. It has a 90-degree left-hand turn at the bottom of the hill, and as you are getting close to it, and thinking you should be slowing down some time soon, the track drops off a little more, making you go faster and making the bike a little lighter, taking traction away! It puts butterflies in your stomach every time, especially if you are trying out-brake someone into the turn. There is also a fast sweeping right-hand turn called "Canada Corner" that is very off-camber and requires a lot of skill and focus to get it just right.

Race tracks are never known for gourmet cuisine. Usually, an edible hamburger is the best you can hope for. Not so for Elkhart Lake. The VFW has the food concession (or they did back then), and they made the best bratwurst in the world. You could smell it all over the track, and it always had everyone salivating.

Early June was a very nice time to be there. Pleasant during the day, and a little cool in the evening. I got in on Friday evening and met the team at Schultz's Lakeside Resort, about the only decent place to stay short of commuting from Milwaukee. They were feeling pretty good about the bikes after Friday practice. On Saturday, we qualified well with the 250, but had a disaster with the 500, which had a transmission failure in the heat race and DNF (Did Not Finish). We frantically worked on the bike while Ron Barrick pleaded with the AMA to at least allow Randy to start last. Technically, he failed to qualify, but there is a provision for "Promoter's Option" to let a nonqualifier start the race.

Kork Ballington wasn't riding a 250 that weekend, so Don Green and Rich Oliver were the main competitors. Don Green's bike developed a cylinder base gasket leak, and Randy just outrode Rich Oliver to take the checkered flag! Not much time to celebrate, though, because we were still getting the 500 ready for the feature race.

Randy started about 30th (last) and made quick work of the tail-end bikes. He was soon into the top 10, but now he's racing guys who are pretty dang fast. He got by Miles Baldwin on a TZ750, then Wes Cooley on an RS500 and Russel Polk on another. Wayne Rainey and Kork Ballington were pretty far ahead by then, but Randy managed to take 3rd place. Not bad for starting last! Kork won and took the lead in the championship.

Loudon, NH

Its official name is Bryar Motorsport Park, but everybody just calls it Loudon, unless, as they sometimes do, they are running the track backwards.

Then it is known as "Noduol." Confoundingly, it is actually located in Laconia, NH, and the weekend is called the Laconia Motorcycle Classic! It is a very short, tight circuit with about 11 turns in 1.5 miles. So, you are turning almost all the time, with short straight sections connecting the turns. It is hard on brakes and getting a quick lap time is very technical. The locals who race it several times a year are always quickest on Friday. The most exciting feature is a hill that you crest going pretty quickly with a hard right-hand turn at the bottom. Some riders would stand the bike up on the front wheel under braking here. Getting traction off of the tight turns is crucial, so tires play an important role.

The track is not too far from where I lived in Connecticut, so I was able to drive there on Friday evening. I got to know the Honda support truck guys that weekend. Udo Geitl was the team manager. He was famous for having managed the BMW roadrace team, which had won several AMA Superbike championships, despite racing with what should have been slower machinery. But they beat the much faster Hondas often by just being more reliable. Honda hired Udo with the mission of making Honda's racebikes reliable. Brian Uchida was in charge of parts, which took up a lot of space in the semitruck rig that they brought to all the races. Brian's main job was to support all the independent Honda-mounted competitors, and he was a really helpful guy.

Kork Ballington was a nice, affable Australian guy. We would talk between practice sessions and tell jokes, etc. His brother was his mechanic, who always had jokes to tell. At the end of a day's running, he liked to remove the cylinders from the engine "to give the pistons a little sunshine." Kork's bike was the same as ours, so we liked to see what his engine looked like.

The Honda RS250 was the best bike to have that year for F2. Some people still rode Yamahas, and Yamaha had not given up the class by any means, but in 1986, the Honda had some advantages, and as soon as it's clear that one race bike is the fastest, all the fast guys immediately get that bike, so its dominance is a fait accompli. They had one odd design feature, both expansion chambers (exhaust pipes) come up the right side of the bike. So, if you fell on that side, you trashed two expensive parts. Brian Uchida knew to stock plenty of them. When you heard that somebody had fallen in practice, your first question was, "Which side?" Then you inquired if the rider was okay.

In F1, Randy beat Kork Ballington and Wayne Rainey to take the win in a closely contested race with lots of turn-to-turn passes and fairing rubbing. In the F2 race, Randy was involved in a front-running pack until he low-sided hard at the bottom of the hill. He slid for a while on his right hand and abraded a lot of skin off of his knuckles. When we got the bike back to the pits, Jim Allen from Dunlop was right there, wanting to know what happened. Randy said the front tire just let loose unexpectedly. We had put on brand new tires just before the race, so Jim wanted to have a look at them. Dunlop took the front tire and cut it up to thoroughly inspect it. He came back to our pits almost in tears. He said it was the wrong compound tire, and that's why Randy fell. His crew had mixed up the tire compounds and installed a much harder compound tire with less traction than what Randy had been practicing on. Jim took complete responsibility for the crash. A sad end to an otherwise excellent weekend.

Pocono, PA

We came to Pocono leading F1, but having scored zero points in F2, we were back to 3rd place.

Pocono is one of several east coast tracks (Daytona, Charlotte, etc.) that have a large oval for stock car and Indy car racing, and a roadrace course for sports car and motorcycle racing. The Pocono oval has relatively shallow banking and, in roadrace configuration, you run the oval in the opposite direction that the stock cars and Indy cars do. So, you go around the oval clockwise, with the infield on your right. You head into the infield section right after going by the pits, with seven turns before going back onto the banking about three-fourths the way around. There is a quick chicane that takes off and back onto the oval, then you go around the banking and back onto the pit straight. There is usually a wind blowing in your face down the pit straight, which makes drafting an important strategy for carrying speed.

Randy's right hand was still in bad shape from his Loudon crash. Putting a glove on was painful, so he took adhesive tape and scissors, and cut little triangular shaped pieces of tape that just fit on his knuckles where the skin was worn off. This left him with flexibility in his hand, but cushioned the abrasion between the glove and his raw skin.

In Friday practice, he had found some slippery spots on the track where the pavement was worn smooth by the stock car tires. So, in the evening, he walked the entire track carrying a can of white spray paint. When he found a slippery spot, he painted a big white spot on it so he could see it while he was riding. A slippery spot doesn't really matter if you are going straight, but it matters a lot if you are turning or braking hard.

Things went to hell right off the bat with the 250. I had rebuilt the engine in between races, and Randy ran a few break-in laps before opening it up. As soon as he wound it out on the oval, one of the cylinders seized up, and he had to coast back into the pits. Cylinders off, it was obvious that the mixture was too lean. Looking at the carburetors, we had the same jetting as for Loudon, a very different track that didn't have any long straightaways. I was in charge of the 250, so it was my fault. Off to the Honda truck to get a new piston and cylinder and put the bike back together…and rejet the carburetors!

At Pocono, you have a real garage to work in, with its own electricity and air compressor…quite luxurious! Later that afternoon, we were working away, and we heard a bike fire up in the garage behind ours that sounded very strange. It was really loud, it idled at about 4,000 RPM, and when they revved it up, the response was astonishingly fast. We stopped what we were doing to walk around and see what this was. It was a top fuel motorcycle drag racer. It was about twice as long as a normal motorcycle, with a big supercharger taking up much of that length, and a wrinkle-wall slick rear tire that was huge. Pocono also has a one-eighth mile drag strip, and they were having drag races in the evening, after we were done.

Randy qualified 2nd on the 500, but not so well on the 250. With the missed practice time it was still jetted a little too rich and some of the other bikes were quicker.

Come Sunday morning, Randy went out for the morning shakedown run on the 500 and pulled back in the pits right away looking frantic. He said the crankshaft did not sound right, and that we had to change engines. We only had about three hours before the race, so we really had to hustle.

Pocono was the closest race to Virginia and Maryland, and a lot of our old WERA buddies had come up for the race. Unfortunately, they were hanging out in our garage, and they wanted to help. Ron Barrick and I knew we had no time to waste, and that he and I could do the job much quicker if no one else was in the way, so we had to throw everyone out unceremoniously. We got the job done with little time to spare. There is always an uneasy feeling when you know you've done everything right, but you haven't had time to properly shake it down and verify everything.

Randy got 3rd off the line and passed Kork Ballington with a drafting slingshot coming by the pits at the end of the first lap (I guess Australians don't learn about drafting the way Americans do!). Then he followed Wayne Rainey for several laps before passing him on the inside into to turn one, going into the infield. They had an amazingly close race, with Randy leading by a little on the last lap, and Wayne setting up for a drafting maneuver. Coming off the banking onto the pit straight Wayne was right behind Randy, and Randy swerved hard in both directions, trying to get Wayne out of his draft. Wayne followed him and was never in a position to slingshot Randy. Randy crossed the finish line a bike length ahead to win! On the podium, Randy asked Wayne, "Why did you follow me, and not just go straight?" This was a little payback for the race that Randy had lost to Mike Baldwin on the same track under similar conditions.

Randy ran well in the 250 race, but finished 3rd behind Don Green, with Rich Oliver taking his first ever win in the class.

Mid-Ohio Raceway

I missed a couple of races because of work, so the next time I was with the team was at Mid-Ohio Raceway in Lexington, OH, in the middle of beautiful Ohio countryside. The various championships were shaping up with Randy and Kork Ballington left as the contenders in F1. Wayne Rainey decided to forego the F1 race in order to focus on Superbikes, where he had a very good shot at the championship, and Randy decided to sit out the F2 race to focus on F1. So Ron Barrick, Doc Bigoney, and I were all focused on the RS500.

Everything went smoothly in practice and qualifying and Randy got a great holeshot to start the race. Kork followed a few seconds behind, biding his time, and knowing that 2nd place would at least carry the championship over to the last race at Road Atlanta. There is a right/left juke before you come onto the pit straight, and getting a good drive out of that juke is what gives you speed down the straight. About three-quarters the way through the race, Kork got on it a little too soon and low-sided in the left hander. It wasn't a hard crash, and he was back up in a second, but his bike was too damaged to carry on. Ron and I hung out the pit board for Randy – "#99 OUT" (Kork was #99, Randy was #96). Randy knew that meant that all he had to do was to stroke the bike home and he was 1986 F1 Champion. About 10 nail-biting laps later, he crossed the finish line in 1st, and that was it! Another national championship for Randy, and all of his friends who raced vicariously through him.

BTW – Wayne Rainey crashed in the Superbike race, leaving that championship to Sam McDonald. Wayne, however, went on to dominate the 1987 Superbike season. He eventually went to race in Europe and was two-time World Champion before a tragic crash left him paralyzed from the waist down.

I thought about the guys Randy had raced and beaten and it was pretty impressive. I also thought about how many seemed to be full-time racers with no apparent source of income. Randy continued to work at Cycle Sport, and then at Fitness Resource, a new business owned by Cycle Sport, the entire time he was racing. He bought his own bikes and parts, excepting the RS250 that Don McLean had loaned him and, since 1984, sponsorship money from Starfire Insurance. Of course, this was professional racing, and there was substantial prize money involved, but he earned what he won. I don't want to name names, but as an example, Don Green (Don – forgive me if I am wrong about this) always had two brand new race bikes. He raced club races on non-AMA weekends, and he raced motocross if nothing else was going on. Near as I could tell, he didn't have a job, so it seemed that he had his own source of money. And there were a lot of guys like that. Not that I wouldn't take that situation if it were mine, and I don't begrudge it to anyone, but that was certainly not Randy's situation. His success was due to his own hard work and determination.

CHAPTER 9
1987

A lot changed in 1987. The AMA, in their wisdom, decided to end the Formula 1 class and focus on superbikes. Their logic was that they would get more support from the manufacturers if the bikes looked more like the street bikes that ordinary people could buy and ride. It was good logic, and Suzuki, who hadn't been directly involved with roadracing in the U.S., decided to put together an AMA Superbike program using their GSXR750 sportbike, which was wonderfully light and quick, if not totally reliable. They hired Vance & Hines, multiple time motorcycle drag racing championship winners, to run the program. Terry Vance was the drag racer and Byron Hines was the engine builder. They were always extremely professional and were certainly capable of making a fast bike. They hired Randy to ride for them.

As for me, I noticed that I was getting fewer and fewer students for my classes at the technical training center, as the motorcycle business in general was slowing down. On the other hand, Honda's auto business was growing by leaps and bounds, and they had just launched the Acura Division. Rather than wait for the motorcycle division to reassign me to North Dakota, I took a job with Auto

Service Training in California, which was a promotion as well. That meant I was pretty busy with relocation and learning a new job.

However, I did make it to a couple of Randy-Races that year.

Road Atlanta

Randy was riding the Vance & Hines Suzuki in Superbike class, which was now the featured class. Since he was Formula 1 Champion from 1986, they allowed him to run a #1 plate with an "F" suffix. So, he was "1F." Vance & Hines provided him with three mechanics for that bike and they didn't need Ron and I, but Randy was also riding a new Honda RS250 in the F2 class, painted in Vance & Hines colors. They provided uniforms for Ron Barrick and I, so we could work on the 250 and look like official members of the team.

Road Atlanta, like most of the really cool race tracks in the world, is built on a hillside, and there is a lot of elevation change. It goes from a pit straight at the bottom of the hill, up the hill, then back down through a series of "esses" then back up and onto a very long back straight that eventually goes down steeply into a left-right switchback that leads back up the hill into a blind, right, steep-down-hill sweeper that leads back onto the pit straight. That is turn 12, and it is challenging in that you have be set up for it before you can see it, and your speed through it is what gives you your drive down the pit straight. If you do it well, you are sliding some as you settle onto the flat pit straight.

I was watching Randy do exactly that in practice on the 250, the bike sliding and wiggling as he came onto the straight. When he came into the pits, he asked me what alternate gear ratios we had for 3rd and 4th gears. He said he was going through the turn at 12,500 RPM and had to shift to 4th in the middle of the turn. He'd rather be at about 11,000 RPM in 3rd and shift into 4th once the bike was headed down the straightaway. I immediately thought "You son-of-a-bitch! While your bike is sliding and twitching, you are looking at the tachometer!" I would be far too busy looking at the track and controlling the bike to even think about that!

We had the alternate gear ratios he wanted, but changing gear ratios required removing the engine, so we did it that night.

The Superbike was fast and light, so light that they ballasted it by putting wheel weights in the exhaust system to get it through tech inspection. After inspection, they took the weights back out, making it technically illegal. The engine was powerful, but it was tuned like a drag bike, with a very steep torque curve, so the power came on quite suddenly when it reached the right RPM, and the lightweight chassis flexed quite a lot when the power hit in the middle of the turn, making it a difficult bike to ride. Randy struggled with it in practice and spent a lot of time talking with the Vance & Hines mechanics about how to tame the power delivery. As a rider, you like to reach the limit of traction in a smooth, progressive way so you can manage the power vs traction curve and keep it at the limit, but not too far beyond it. When the power comes on too suddenly, the rear wheel breaks loose into a slide, and the chassis flexes, causing the bike to wobble. About all the rider can do at that point is to back off until you have the bike back under control.

Qualifying was on Saturday afternoon, with the 250 race immediately following Superbike heat races. Randy qualified the 250 on the front row.

After lunch, he went out in his Superbike heat race. On the 2nd lap, he got into an uncontrollable wobble going onto the back straight and crashed heavily enough to cause a red flag. Randy was taken to the track medical clinic, and the mangled superbike was trucked back to the pits. With the 250 race coming right up, Ron Barrick and I decided that I would warm up the bike and push it out to the grid while he went to the clinic to pick up Randy. He brought a roll of duct tape to patch up Randy's leathers.

I waited on the grid while all the other riders mounted up, put on their helmets, gloves, etc....still waiting. Finally, Ron shows up in a golf cart with Randy. He is bunged up and sore, but functional. We help him get on the bike and get his helmet and gloves on, then we get off the grid just in time for the start.

Randy got one of his patented holeshots and led the race from start to finish!

After the race, Randy was changing out of his leathers in the van, and a couple of officials from the AMA came up to me. I hollered into the van to Randy, and he asked what they wanted. I replied: "They want to measure your testicles. They think they might be illegal!"

The Vance & Hines mechanics were busily repairing the Superbike for tomorrow's main event. Ron and I offered to help, but they didn't really need us, so I went home that night. Randy failed to finish the main event.

The Grand Prix of the United States at Laguna Seca, CA

Randy had negotiated with Vance & Hines to pay for him to bring the RS250 to Laguna Seca in July for the Grand Prix of the United States. This event was part of the world championship series, and the riders who primarily competed in Europe and had full factory support were there. To do well here carries a lot of prestige, even if you are not competing in the full series. They were running two classes: 250cc and 500cc. Randy had run his RS500 in this event before with limited success.

Laguna Seca is near Monterey, CA, a very picturesque town, and the track is one of the coolest in the country, with facilities commensurate with a world championship event. The track is 2.1 miles long with 11 turns. It is laid out on a hillside (as are all the cool racetracks). The pit straight leads up a hill, then plunges down the hill into a difficult hairpin turn to the left. There are two right hand turns and then turn five leads back up a steep hill into a left hander that is hard to get just right, because it drops down into a little gulley right at the apex of the turn. You have to accelerate hard into the turn to have any traction through the turn. Then you head back up the hill again and you finally reach the famous "Corkscrew," a steep downhill left-right juke that is completely blind as you approach it. It looks as though you are falling off the end of the Earth as you make the left hand turn. It is the signature feature of Laguna Seca, and to get the turn sequence just right is very difficult. Next you go through a fast, downhill left-hand sweeper, a right hander, and then left back onto the pit straight. A perfect lap at Laguna Seca is a real accomplishment, and the California guys who race it regularly have a distinct advantage.

I flew out Friday night into San Francisco airport and found that my luggage had not made the trip with me. So, I got to the hotel with my coat and tie and my wingtip shoes to wear the next day. They had a Vance & Hines uniform for me, but no shoes and no clean undies! We ran practice and got a lot of help from Jim Allen, the Dunlop guy. Randy was quick, but the factory race bikes were much quicker than his customer RS250, and the factory riders got special tires that were not available to us. Jim Allen would have gladly given them to us, but they simply didn't have enough of them, and they had strict contracts with the factory teams.

Somehow, Jimmy Felice, who was a California native, had managed to get a one-off ride on a factory Yamaha 250. Jimmy was a Laguna Seca expert, being local and having hundreds and hundreds of laps under his belt.

We practiced and fine-tuned the bike and worked with Jim Allen to find which of the customer tires were the quickest. One of my old friends from the D.C. area, Rob Worrell, came through the pits. We had learned to ride and work on motorcycles together in Virginia, and he was now a BMW mechanic in California. He remarked on my stylish wingtip shoes with the Vance & Hines uniform…said the combination looked very clown-like! Thanks Rob!

I was able to blaze to the airport and pick up my luggage that afternoon. I got back in time for happy hour at the hotel with Jim Allen buying!

Sunday was intense. Randy got a great start, but he was racing the best riders in the world, and those guys had faster bikes. Randy rode hard and ended up in 6th place, first non-factory bike and ahead of a lot of the factory bikes. We all felt pretty good about the result.

Jimmy Felice, friend and local favorite, won the race! It got him a lot of attention, but not a regular factory ride.

My wife flew into SFO that evening, and we headed off on a little summer vacation to visit her friends in L.A. and her cousin in Paso Robles, who owned a vineyard. At this point, we did not yet know that we would be moving to California in the fall!

Randy's Superbike season was pretty miserable, with a lot of DNFs.

CHAPTER 10

I had started my job in California in October, and I lived at the Residence Inn in Torrance, CA, for a couple of months until we found a house in San Pedro, CA. My wife moved out to join me in December of 1987. Randy came out and stayed with us for much of January while he worked with Vance & Hines in Santa Fe Springs, CA, and did testing at Willow Springs Raceway, about two hours away. Randy filled in a major gap in my cultural knowledge by renting the movie "Top Gun" for us to watch one evening. I learned the origin of the phrase, "I feel the need for speed."

Vance & Hines made the bike a lot better for the 1988 season, and Randy managed to take one 3rd place and several 4th places. I was very busy with my new job, and I only saw him when he was in California for testing. He usually stayed at our house in San Pedro. We'd go out to dinner, drink wine, and talk about his adventures and my job with Honda.

Randy told me about racing in the Macau Grand Prix, an invitational race on the island of Macau, near Hong Kong. They paid for Randy to bring his RS500, and he and Ron Barrick made the trip. The island's main business is gambling, and there is a lot of money there. The event brings in throngs of tourists and they pay the riders "show money" (just for showing up!) and significant prize money.

Randy said the island is very crowded, and storefront businesses and repair shops do a lot of their work right on the sidewalk in front. He said he had to walk around various engines and other machinery being repaired on the sidewalk.

1989

Suzuki brought their roadrace team in house for the 1989 season and hired a young, fast kid named Kevin Schwantz to ride for them. Randy told me that he had raced with Kevin Schwantz before, and that he was just loose and sliding all the time, looking like a crash waiting to happen. But it didn't happen! (At least most of the time.)

Randy, in the meantime, was in talks with Honda. Honda was putting together a factory-backed program to be run by Commonwealth Racing, out of Kentucky, which was owned by an entrepreneur named Martin Adams. The plan was to contest the "Battle of the Twins" class with a Honda RS750.

To understand the Battle of the Twins, you need to go back to the AMA's roots. The organization was founded to support and promote the enjoyment of motorcycles in the United States, and there was only one American motorcycle manufacturer: Harley-Davidson. Thus, the AMA and HarleyDavidson were inextricably intertwined. As motorcycle racing became an important part of the organization, it was coordinated directly with Harley-Davidson. In the late 50s and 60s, most of the racing took place on dirt ovals. It was known as "flat-track" racing. It often took place on horse racing tracks, and the bikes slid sideways through the turns, throwing up dirt, making a lot of noise and generally entertaining the fans of the day. The race bikes were mostly Harleys, but there were British bikes that were quick, notably Triumph and BSA. As they began to win races, the AMA modified the rules so that "Overhead Valve" engine bikes were limited to 500cc while flathead engines (the Harley-Davidsons of the time) could be 750cc, effectively giving Harley a 50 percent displacement advantage.

The street Harley-Davidsons had already adopted overhead valve technology, and as soon as the OHV Harley racing bikes got to be quick, the rules were modified again to allow 750cc OHV engines.

Fast forward to the 70s, and roadracing and motocross are becoming very popular, and the Japanese brands are getting to be very good. Harley-Davidson was still dominant in flat-track racing, but that was becoming less and less relevant. By the mid-80s, Harley-Davidson was not competitive in any class of AMA racing when it was still the only American manufacturer supporting the AMA. So, the Battle of the Twins was born. The rules limited bikes to 2-cylinder, 4-stroke engines with displacement advantages for pushrod engines (Harleys) and an open invitation to take your flat-track bike and modify it to be a roadrace bike.

Ducatis were twins and were very good roadracing bikes, but they were limited to 750cc while the Harleys could run 1000cc. A lot of the AMA race fans were Harley-Davidson riders, and the series was very popular with them as Harleys almost always won. These people were tired of their AMA being dominated by "rice-burners" and wanted some good old American iron to have a chance at winning.

The popularity of the series was noticed by Honda and others, and Honda devised a scheme to make a competitive bike, enter it discreetly via Commonwealth Racing, and try to win the series. The plan worked perfectly. The bike was loosely based on a street bike, but with a purpose built V-twin racing engine made by Honda R&D. It was maintained by Ray Plumb of the Honda roadrace team, but always entered by Commonwealth Racing. It dominated the series and took the championship with Randy riding.

I only got to the event at Willow Springs that year, where Randy won and clinched the championship. I was just there as a spectator, but I got into the pits for the celebration! Randy had now won three AMA championships… one every three years!

It got the attention of the Honda roadrace team for the coming year. After a couple years off, they were ready to go back to Superbike racing with a factory effort, and they wanted Randy to ride!

CHAPTER II
1990

I was super busy at work with the introduction of the Acura NSX sports car. I spent three weeks in Japan with the Honda Overseas Training group, then came home and prepared the technical training curriculum for all the Acura dealers (me and my colleagues, that is).

But Randy was in California pretty regularly that year and usually stayed with us. He told me about Daytona, where he missed winning by a tiny margin. He also told me about groupies and autograph signing sessions where girls would ask him to sign their t-shirts, while they were wearing them! These were our fantasies when we were young guys!

The 24 Hours of Willow Springs

WERA ran an endurance racing series that I used participate in when I was riding. One of the feature races on the calendar each year was the Willow Springs 24-hour race that would get coverage in the big motorcycle magazines. I lived in Washington D.C. then and never dreamed of making it to Willow Springs.

In 1990, Dirk Vandenburg, Marketing Manager for the Honda Motorcycle Division decided that we should contest the race with a Honda RC30, a street legal bike that was built exactly for this type of racing, and that was being made available for sale in the U.S. in very limited quantities. He secured a bike from HRC (Honda Racing Corporation) and put together a rider team of Randy Renfrow, Mike Spencer (a former Honda team rider who now worked in Acura PR) and a young California kid who was up-and-coming (I can't remember his name). Dirk knew the people around the office who had pit crew experience, and I was conscripted to help.

Ray Plumb was designated team manager, and we practiced pit stops behind the engineering shops at work the week before the race. The bike was a dream. It had a single-sided swingarm, so you could change the rear wheel in about five seconds (vs 20 seconds for a conventional bike). It was a 750cc V4 that was powerful, but also very reliable with a heavy-duty transmission (often the weak point in endurance racing). And the brake calipers were designed so you could change brake pads very quickly. It had a dry-break fuel filler valve, so refueling was really quick. It was the perfect bike for this race.

At the race track, we had a lot of Honda personnel involved— too many in fact. It looked as though every other person in the pits had a Honda shirt on, and it generated a little resentment from some of the regular teams that contested the whole series.

Willow Springs is in the Mojave Desert out in the middle of nowhere. The nearest town, Rosamond, has a little Mexican restaurant and a small, seedy motel. The nearest town of any size is Lancaster, about 20 miles away on the Antelope Valley Freeway (CA14). It has real hotels and decent restaurants. A little further that direction (toward L.A.) is Palmdale. You are still 100 miles from Los Angeles!

The track is set on a hillside with a long pit straight that leads into a left-right sequence that takes you into a series of esses up a pretty steep hill. There is a right-hand turn at the top of the hill that you have to apex very late in order to be pointed in the right direction going down the hill. At the bottom, turn six is a very off camber left hander that sends you back up the hill to a right-hand turn that leads onto the back straight. The six-seven turn sequence is what determines how good a drive you get onto the back straight, and it is difficult to get right. The back straight leads into a 180-degree carousel that leads you back to the pit straight. It can be tricky because a strong gust of desert wind can catch you as you are all leaned over, and try to stand you up and blow you off the outside of the track! All in all, it is a very cool track that you would not expect to find out in the hinterlands of the desert.

The WERA endurance series was dominated by a team that had support from Suzuki. The team leader was a guy named John Ulrich, who was also editor of *Cycle News*, a weekly enthusiast publication that was mostly devoted to covering race results from the weekend before. John Ulrich had taken over as editor in 1986, and immediately polarized the readership with his opinionated and outspoken views. He called things as he saw them, for better or worse, and we knew that he would have something to say about our Willow Springs effort!

The race started smoothly with Randy riding the first leg. We had calculated how long we could go on a tank of gas, and changed riders every hour or so. I did most of the refueling. The gas can was a large metal cylinder with a cone at the bottom, and the valve that engaged the dry-break valve at the bottom of the cone. It had handles on either side, and it was pretty heavy when it was full of fuel. I would stand on the track side of the pit wall. As the rider was coming in, someone would hand me the tank from over the pit wall. Someone else would steady the bike from the back while the one rider was getting off. Rider off, I could lower the tank onto the dry-break valve and watch the telltale hose on the left of the tank. When I saw that no more fuel was going in, I would lift it up and away, and hand it back over the pit wall. As soon as the tank cleared the bike, the new rider could get on and head back out. All told it took about 15 seconds! Ray Plumb supervised from the pit wall, ready to help or intervene if needed.

I worked most of the night. It was pretty cool watching the bikes come onto the pit straight from the carousel, their lights shining through the darkness. You come out of that turn going pretty quickly already, then accelerate as hard as you can down the straight. The bikes were nearing redline in 6th gear as they came by the pits, riders all tucked in going as fast as they could. Then Randy would come on to the straight. You couldn't see him right away, but you could hear that the RC30's V4 engine sounded distinctly different from the other, mostly inline 4-cylinder bikes. And you could also see Randy blow by the other guys, going about 20 MPH faster than almost anyone else, and braking into turn one much later than them.

By dawn, we were comfortably in the lead by several laps, and I took the opportunity to lay down in my car and take a nap for a couple of hours. When I got up, I saw our bike being unloaded off a truck, very mangled. Ray Plumb threw a tarp over it to keep it from being photographed for the magazines. Our young rider, whose name I can't remember (just as well) had crashed heavily, and the bike was damaged beyond repair. The rider was bunged up enough to be sent to the hospital, but he was basically okay.

We packed things up, then headed home for some sleep.

I finally got to watch a Superbike race at Willow Springs at the end of the season, where Randy won the race over Doug Chandler, the championship leader. On the podium, he thanked me for helping him get started in roadracing. Very nice! And a good way to lead into the next season.

CHAPTER 12
1991

The year started with great excitement as it was announced that Camel cigarettes would sponsor the team on a multi-year contract. Commonwealth Racing became Smokin' Joe's Honda with a much bigger budget than before.

Randy was spending more time in California, meeting with the sponsors and Honda executives and getting ready for the new bike. Finally, in early February, they took the bike out to Willow Springs to shake it down. That's when Randy had a really bad crash in the carousel. A big gust of wind caught him when he was sliding the bike, and he fell and slid at high speed with his weight on his right hand. It literally ground off his thumb and the ends of his right forefinger and middle finger. He also suffered some major tissue trauma to his left calf muscle. They rushed him to the hospital in Lancaster, where they relieved the pressure in his calf and evaluated the hand damage. I drove out to the hospital that evening, and Randy told me what had happened. The plan was for him to be transferred to UCLA hospital, where they would graft his right big toe onto his right hand to replace his thumb! They actually wanted to use the left big toe, but Randy insisted on using the right one, because you really need the left one for shifting gears. The right one is involved in applying the rear brake, but it's nowhere near as crucial.

After his surgery at UCLA, Randy came to our house in San Pedro to recuperate. The toe/thumb looked a little weird, but it functioned pretty well as a thumb. The end knuckle didn't articulate, but it he could grip things normally.

They also installed a turnbuckle apparatus on each of his two damaged fingers. Their purpose was to stretch them! They looked like miniature versions of a medieval torture device. They had pins that went into the bone, and a thumb screw that he was to turn periodically to maintain stretching force on the bone. It had to be painful, but Randy was still in "The Order of the Broken Crutch," and he seemed to be able to manage pain without letting it slow him down. He eventually gained a few millimeters of length in each finger, enough to let him reach the front brake lever.

The accident completely ruined the Smokin' Joe's Honda's plans. There was no way Randy could be ready to ride by Daytona, and the rest of the season was dubious, so Honda hired Miguel Duhamel to take Randy's place. Miguel was young and fast, and was the son of a famous Canadian rider named Yvon Duhamel, who had the distinction of being the first one to exceed 150 MPH at Daytona on a motorcycle.

Randy stayed with us through February. He came to dinner with us to celebrate my 40th birthday at my favorite French restaurant called J'Adore, and we shared a magnum of 1966 Chateau Ducru Beaucaillou that was wonderful! Then he went back to Virginia to focus on the Fitness Resource business for the summer.

It was a busy year for me. I had a two-week trip to Japan for 1991 Acura Legend training. Then my wife asked me to leave, so I moved to an apartment in Long Beach. We got divorced soon after. I took up with one of my wine tasting friends, and we eventually got married, after dealing with divorces on both sides. We bought a house in Palos Verdes the following May, where we still live.

CHAPTER 13
1992

I kept in touch with Randy. I had another business trip to Japan in June, and it turned out that it coincided with the 8-Hours of Suzuka. Randy was riding for an independent Japanese dealer group on a Honda VFR750, teamed with a racing buddy of his named Dale Quarterly.

The 8-Hours of Suzuka is part of a worldwide endurance racing series, and it is a huge event in Japan. The Japanese are incredible race fans, and motorcycle racing has a bigger fan base than auto racing. There is a Motorcycle Grand Prix of Japan, but the 8-Hours of Suzuka is even more important to them, with a whole week of practice and events leading up to the race. To race in that event makes you a big celebrity, regardless of how you do.

It is held on a facility that is entirely owned by Honda. It includes an amusement park with a Ferris wheel, and there is a resort hotel on the property. The race track is fast and challenging, and it has the distinction of being the only international circuit that crosses over itself.

My business meeting started the Monday after the race, so I booked my flights to get into Tokyo on Friday evening. I would check into my hotel in Ikebukuro, then get up early Saturday morning and head to Suzuka. I consulted with a friend at work, Dave Fender, who had been there before. Dave apparently had the best job in the world. You could always find him in the cafeteria. He is British by origin, and he managed to arrange business trips so that he could go to Wimbledon every year, and to the Isle of Man TT every year. He managed to get to Suzuka sometimes, but not this year. But he knew what trains to take, where to get a taxi, and how to get to the track hotel, which is where I was to meet Randy.

Flying into Japan, where the time is 16 hours earlier than L.A., is a challenge in time management. If you sleep on the plane, you will not sleep when you get to Japan. So, you try to stay awake for the whole flight. I would chat up the flight attendants, walk up and down the aisles, and drink heavily, but not so much that it put me to sleep. Honda paid for business class for international flights, and I always tried to get the upper deck on a 747. There was plenty of room to do push-ups on the floor, and pull-ups on the stair railing. In those days, there was a smoking section at the back of the upstairs lounge. That's where all the Japanese executives would be.

At Narita airport, there is a "Limousine Bus" (more bus than limousine) that will take you directly to your hotel in Tokyo, about a two-hour ride. Tough to stay awake, but I did my best. Once at the hotel and settled in, I forced myself to have dinner, even though I wasn't at all hungry. But if you don't do it, then your digestive system never gets onto Japan time. My hotel had a nice French restaurant called "Le Mistral." Dinner and a bottle of wine would put me to sleep, regardless of what time my body thought it was.

I was up at 5:00 AM to catch the train. Trains in Japan are amazing, and when you get onto the Shinkansen (the bullet train), it is truly amazing. It's about a four-hour trip altogether, but the Shinkansen covers the last 150 miles in a little over an hour in complete comfort. Taxis are waiting at the train station, and I had my instructions written out in Japanese for the taxi driver. At the track hotel, the desk clerks spoke pretty good English. I asked them to contact the Sakurai Racing Team's pit garage. They told me to have a seat in the lobby, and someone would be right with me. In about 10 minutes, Randy walks in, takes me out to his scooter, and we go blazing through a huge crowd of people in the pit area. There was barely room to move, it was so crowded, but they somehow parted like the red sea to let Randy and I through.

In the pits, I met the crew. They didn't speak much English, but I knew enough Japanese to manage, so we made friends. I also met Dale Quarterly for the first time. Dale is a tall, lanky guy with carrot-red hair. He was well over six-feet and at least a foot taller than Randy. It's amazing that they were able to set a bike up, so they both could ride it. The team had made a cute sticker depicting their two riders, except that Randy was standing on a stool, so he could get his head somewhere near Dale's. Dale was a nice guy and a good rider. He could go out on a track and be up to full speed in just a couple of laps. Randy would always work up to it, each lap faster than the one before. In the end, Randy was the faster of the two, but they made a good team.

Qualifying was already done when I got there. Randy told me it is so intense, that when it is over the pit crews spontaneously applaud, just because they can now pause to breathe. We headed to the track hotel where there was a post-qualifying reception that included a ceremony with sake for everyone, and a mass "Kampai!" toast. I crashed in Randy's room, having brought a toothbrush and a change of underwear with me.

Sunday morning, we were back on the scooter weaving through incredible throngs of spectators to get to the pits. In the morning warm-up, I found that I could make myself useful translating Randy's input to the mechanics. I was also made to understand that Randy's lower intestinal tract was not happy, and that he needed to be close to the bathroom.

Randy rode the first stint in the race, and when he came in to change riders, he disappeared quickly, and the pit crew guys turned to me, "Randy wa doko desuka?" (Where is Randy?).

"Otearai," I responded (bathroom), and one of them headed off to the men's room to talk to Randy while he was in his stall!

Randy and Dale rode well, and came in first non-factory supported team, a fact that was fully understood by the fans and made them stars, despite being a long way from the podium.

I needed to get back to Tokyo, and Dale and his girlfriend needed to catch a flight home that evening. Randy was staying the night at the track hotel, so he asked me if I would help Dale and his girlfriend to get on the train and off at the airport. No problem for an experienced traveler like me! We get to the crowded train station and 6'2", red-haired Dale is like some kind of mythical dragon in their midst, towering above everyone else. He also has a luggage kit that is huge, and will not fit through the turnstile. He and I lift it up and over, as the crowd watched in amazement! On the train, there are fans who know who he is, and ask for his autograph. They ask for mine, too, just because I am with him and might actually be somebody.

We reach the stop for the airport and say goodbye, everyone exhausted at this point. I get a wonderful night's sleep and am bright-eyed and bushytailed for my business meeting the next morning.

24 Hours of Willow Springs (Reprise)

After years of promoting V4 motorcycles, Honda was bringing out some really good, if more conventional, inline 4-cylinder motorcycles, with the CBR1000R as the fastest, most race-ready in the lineup. Dirk Vandenburg at Honda decided that it was time to have another go at the 24 Hours of Willow Springs, this time with a more focused approach. Ray Plumb still as team manager, and Randy and Mike Spencer as riders, but a smaller, more discreet crew. This being a relatively normal, production bike, he could just take one from inventory and not have to account to HRC for the unit.

It was a wonderful bike, but not specialized like the RC30, meaning tire and brake pad changes were going to take longer. Ray Plumb and I practiced both, trying to figure out how to work together to get the jobs done efficiently. Front brake pads were especially crucial, knowing that the caliper would be really hot when we did it in a live pit stop. The rear tire, unlike the RC30, had a normal,

2-sided swingarm, and the wheel assembly included the rear sprocket and rear brake disc. That meant that you had to pull the cotter pin that retained the nut, remove the nut (with an air-gun), pull out the axle, then put the new wheel assembly in place, aligning the brake disc in between the brake pads, push it forward, so you could get the chain over the sprocket, then pull it backwards, so you could push the axle through the swingarm and wheel bearings. Then the washer and nut could go on, get tightened, cotter pin back in, and off we go, refueling having taken place in the meantime. We got it down to 15 seconds, practicing at Honda behind the engineering shops.

At the track, they had brought an entire spare bike, along with spare wheels, tires, brake pads and all the other stuff we expected to need. Dirk had taken the spare bike from a local dealer's allocation, not expecting to need it.

The favorites were, as usual, the Suzuki…John Ulrich…team. We were about even in practice, and when the race started, we were looking good… on the same lap, but in the lead. Randy was on his second stint when, going up the hill, another bike had a spectacular engine failure, covering the track with oil. Randy was right behind him. He had a low-side crash on the left side of the bike. A lot of other riders crashed as well. The race was red-flagged while they cleaned up the mess, and our bike came back to us on a truck with the left side pretty bunged up, but repairable. We got to work, transferring parts from the spare bike (sorry about that dealer's inventory!)

We lost about an hour getting the bike ready to go out again, and it was beginning to get dark. Ray and I recalculated our tire and brake pad changes. About 10:00 PM, it was time for a new rear tire, and when the bike came into the pits, we got it up on the stand, I pulled the cotter pin and spun off the axle nut. Ray pulled the axle through and our other guys pulled out the wheel/tire assembly and fed in the new one. I finagled the disc into the brake pads, and we pushed the wheel forward while Ray installed the chain onto the sprocket. We pulled the wheel back and Ray got the axle through, me helping to guide it through the swingarm. Now all I had to do was put on the washer and tighten the nut…but I dropped the washer and fumbled around for what seemed like an eternity picking it up and getting it onto the axle…finally…on with the nut. *Brrrrrp!* with the air gun and cotter pin installed, and off wc go! I stood up feeling as though I had completely botched the operation. The guys from the pit wall said, "13 seconds…good job guys!" We almost beat the refueling!

About 3:00 AM, we changed a front tire and replaced front brake pads. You wear special gloves for working with really hot parts, and you handle them gingerly. The front wheel and axle are an assembly, with the two brake rotors included. Our replacement tire was on the entire assembly. Removal was really easy, undoing four nuts on the end of the forks and dropping the assembly down. Now you have to push the caliper pistons back into position for the new brake pads, then remove the really hot old pads. The new pads aren't hot, but the caliper is, so you need to be careful. New pads in place, another team member hands us the new wheel/tire assembly, we get the brake rotors aligned with the brake pads, axle clamps in place, nuts tightened and safety-wired, and off we go!

In the wee hours of the morning, the leading Suzuki team had a timing chain failure! They pitted, and removed the cylinder head. The rules forbid wholesale engine replacements, or even major components, like a cylinder head, so they had to disassemble and repair the cylinder head (bent valves). They were incredibly efficient, but the incident helped us make up the time from the crash. Now there were other, very good teams in the lead, but we were making up time, and we took the lead with about an hour to go. Victory!

Time for beer, handshakes, hugs, etc.… then back home for some sleep.

CHAPTER 14
1994

R andy accepted an offer to ride for a private entry team on a Honda CBR600 (otherwise known as a Honda Hurricane) in a new class for 600cc 4-stroke street-based motorcycles. It was a sort of mini-superbike class that would eventually replace Formula 2. Randy had his own 250 to run in F2. I was again really busy at work, and only made it to one race, at Pomona Fairgrounds in southern California.

Pomona

Pomona was famous for its drag strip, but it was never intended as a roadrace venue. The track was pretty mickey-mouse, with chain link fencing set up to define the track through the parking lot and down the dragstrip. The parking lot surface was breaking up, with loose gravel all over. The AMA chose the location based on the promoter's promise to build a professional facility, and Pomona was much closer to big Southern California population centers than Willow Springs.

I got up early Saturday morning and drove out to Pomona. Randy had a pit credential for me. We met with Ron Barrick, our old friend who was now President of AMA Professional Racing! He and Randy drove around the track and noted places where the condition was bad. They then met with the promoter to get them fixed as best they could at the last minute. Randy was now a sort of senior rider representative, having the respect of everyone there. He had a t-shirt that said: "The older I get, the faster I was."

He had bought a 125cc roadrace bike, just for fun. He said it was so light, that when he did a quick switchback, the whole bike would come off the ground! I helped him prep the 250 and the 125, then went home in time to get to a wine tasting party where my wife was waiting for me.

I got up early again on Sunday morning and headed back to the track. Randy was pretty laid back, just enjoying riding and having fun. It was good to see.

Randy tried to retire. He made an announcement, and *Cycle News* did a big spread on him. He focused on building the Fitness Resource business in Virginia. We stopped by the store to see him a couple of times when I was in D.C. on business.

But he missed the competition, and he came back a couple of times, focusing on 250cc racing. Rich Oliver had become the top guy in that class, and Randy knew he could beat him! Randy had a couple of nasty crashes that put him back into "The Order of the Broken Crutch." When he was hurt, he used to say, "If you want to play, you gotta pay." But he got several more podium finishes at Daytona.

In 2002, he had another crash and was recuperating at his parents' home in Virginia and seemed to be getting better (again!). Apparently, he was coming up the stairs from the basement, on crutches, when he fell over backwards and hit his head on the concrete floor. He later died from the head injury. One of my old WERA buddies from Maryland called me that evening and told me the news. I sent his mom flowers and a card. The card said: "Randy was my hero." I thought about the irony of him dying from falling down the stairs, after having crashed at over 100 MPH a dozen times.

EPILOGUE

We continued to exchange Christmas cards with Randy's mom until she passed away. She was a religious woman, and I'm sure she believed that Randy was in a better place, with no more broken bones and no more pain. She loved her dogs, and Shawn, Randy's younger brother, and would keep us up to date on their news.

I worked pretty closely with Brian Uchida at Honda until I retired, and Brian and I would reminisce about Randy. Brian had made a cute memorial sticker of a Randy cartoon figure.

Randy still shows up in my dreams once in a while. He was an amazing guy and a good friend.

CycleNews.com

The starting line for the Loudon 1986 Formula 1 race.

Wayne Rainey #6 is on Pole. Randy #96 is starting
3rd in the middle of the front row. Kork Ballington
#99 is on the front row to Randy's left.

Larry Lawrence/riderfiles.wordpress.com

**The podium at Loudon, N.H., 1986 after the
feature race with Randy on the top step!**

From left-to-right: Kork Ballington, Trophy girl with
"Miss Loudon" Sash, Woman whose face is covered
by Randy's arm, Randy Renfrow, Wayne Rainey

**Picture taken at Mid-Ohio Raceway immediately after
Randy clinched the 1986 AMA Formula 1 Championship.**

From left-to-right: Ron Barrick (seated on the bike),
Doc Bigoney, Randy Renfrow, Tom Manchester (me)

Randy on the Vance & Hines liveried RS 250

He was thanking my wife (at the time) Maggie
and I for letting him stay at our house a lot.

The sticker that Brian Uchida had made

youtube.com

Randy on the podium at Mid-Ohio 1986, having just clinched the AMA Formula1 National Championship.

He is just about to pop open a bottle of champagne,
and the trophy girls are hoping to not get sprayed!

Photo by Mike 'Stu' Stuhler/Stu's Shots/
Indianapolis stusshots.blogspot.com

Randy at the Mid-Ohio in 1998

canadianmotorcyclehalloffame.ca

Jim Allen - The Dunlop Tire Guy

YAMAHA RD350

A Yamaha RD350 was a 2-cylinder air-cooled 2-stroke motorcycle that was light, quick and reliable. It was, at the time, the culmination of 2-stroke technology development that took 2-stroke engines from being noisy, smoky obnoxious things in the 60s to being seriously fast with the potential to make almost twice the horsepower of a 4-stroke engine of the same displacement. The RD series (250 and 350) was introduced in 1973. They were a step up from Yamaha's previous 2-stroke street bikes with the most important improvement being reed valves in the intake tract. This allowed for a longer intake duration without having a problem with blow-back through the carburetors. They also had a front disc brake and much better suspension.

> *NOTE: Piston engines are generally classified as 2-stroke or 4-stroke. Most people learn the 4-stroke cycle in driver's education because almost all cars use this type of engine:*
> *Intake – piston going down, intake valve open, drawing fuel and air into the cylinder*
> *Compression – piston going up, compressing the mixture in the combustion chamber (both valves closed)*

Power – the spark plug ignites the mixture and the resulting pressure forces the piston downward, applying force to the crankshaft (both valves closed)
Exhaust – piston going up, exhaust valve open, forcing the spent gases out of the cylinder and making room for the cycle to start over again.

In a 2-stroke engine, these events are all accomplished in one upward and one downward piston stroke, using ports in the cylinder wall instead of valves, and using a sealed crankcase and the underside of the piston to pump intake fuel and air from the carburetor to the combustion chamber. Because a 2-stroke engine has a power stroke every time the piston goes downward (as opposed to every other time in a 4-stroke engine), at any given RPM it is making twice as many power strokes, giving it a distinct power advantage, as well as being more compact and much lighter weight thanks to the absence of valves, camshafts and other valve train components.

There are downsides. Because the ports are in the cylinder wall, the full compression stroke is not used, losing a little bit of efficiency. Also because the crankcase is sealed and used for pumping intake air and fuel, the lubrication of the piston, cylinder, and crankshaft bearings is accomplished by mixing oil with the gas. This means there will be oil smoke coming out as the engine runs. This issue led to the eventual demise of the 2-stroke engine as emissions rules became more stringent.

I bought my RD350 in 1974 when I was working as a mechanic in a Suzuki shop in Annandale, VA. It was wrecked, and I bought it for $200. The biggest issue from the wreck was the front forks, which were pretty severely bent. The lower tubes, or sliders as they known, which hold the front wheel axle, were a little dinged up, but otherwise okay. The downtubes, which are clamped into the steering head, were bent about 15 degrees. Thankfully, they are made from mild steel and can be straightened in a hydraulic press. This operation does require some skill in that you don't want to squash the tube and put in dents or flat spots, because the outer surface needs to make a seal against the sliders, so the damping oil in the sliders does not leak. You support the outer ends of the tube while applying pressure from the press at bend point until it is straight—actually, you have to press it a little past straight, because it springs back some when you release the pressure. You then release the press until it is just clear of the fork tube. Then you rotate the tube, sighting against the press to look for runout. If it is straight, the gap will remain the same as you rotate the tube. If the gap varies, you find the high point and press again. When you think you have it perfect, you then put a dial gauge on the bent spot, which allows you to check for runout down to 0.01mm, finer than you can see with your eye. This was my bike, so I got it as perfect as was possible.

The gas tank was dented, so I did my best to beat out the dent and then bondo and sand it to look as good as new. I painted it blue, my favorite color!

The foot pegs were damaged, so I fabricated some rear-set foot pegs using some aluminum stock we had laying around and after-market buddy pegs. Then you flip the shift lever over backwards, so you can reach it with your toe from the rear-set pegs. This accomplishes two things:

The rearset pegs allow you to tuck in better to minimize your wind resistance

The flipped over shift lever changes the direction of upshifts and downshifts

> *NOTE: Normal shift patterns have you push the lever upwards with your toe for an upshift and downwards for a downshift, which seems logical enough. However, the downward pressure on the lever is much more positive than the upward pressure, so you are far less likely to miss an upshift with the pattern reversed. And when you are racing, the upshifts are more crucial. If you miss a downshift under braking, you just repeat it with no time lost, but if you miss an upshift, you lose precious acceleration time, and the guy who was behind you is now in front of you!*

I also installed "Clubman" handlebars, which are narrower and lower than normal bars, which also help you tuck in to reduce wind resistance.

Perhaps you have guessed that this bike was being prepared for racing, roadracing in particular. I had raced motocross for a few years with middling success, but I had a buddy who had taken up roadracing and found that it rewarded tuning and precision over endurance and brute strength as motocross did. There was a "local" race track in West Virginia called Summit Point Raceway and a club called East-Coast Roadracing Association (ERA) ran motorcycle races there during the spring and summer.

NOTE: Roadracing refers to racing held on a closed-circuit race track that has a paved racing surface similar to a public road. Sometimes public roads are closed off to make a temporary roadracing circuit. The most famous example would be the Grand Prix of Monaco for Formula 1 cars. However, Summit Point was a typical closed, dedicated race track that was mostly used for racing sports cars. In the 60s and early 70s, motorcycle roadracing was more popular in Europe than in the United States. In Europe, motorcycles were (still are) a very common form of daily transportation, and ordinary people could relate closely to the competitions. With the gas crisis of 1974, motorcycles became much more popular in the U.S. as a form of daily transportation, and motorcycle roadracing began to catch on as well.

I rode the bike back and forth to work, getting used to the new shift pattern and ergonomics. Finally, I went to my first race at Summit Point. I ran Novice Class 400cc Production (the modifications I had made were allowed in Production Class, and you also removed turn signals and unnecessary street equipment). This being my first race, they made me put a big X on my back with duct tape, so the more experienced riders would know to look out for me! I ran practice, and with some coaching from my friends, I began to get the hang of this type of racing. I also discovered that the class I was running in was huge. There were maybe 300 bikes there for the weekend, prepared to run in various classes. About 100 of them were Yamaha RD250/350s in various stages of modification. It was really a club within a club, because if you needed something for your RD, say, a 13-tooth front sprocket, there were plenty of people who would gladly sell you one, or might even loan it to you. There was a really heartwarming camaraderie where, if someone crashed, all the other RD folks would chip in to try to get the bike fixed in time to race, even if it belonged to your competitor. We'd settle up about the parts later.

The time for my first race came, and because I was new, I was gridded at the back. In those days we were gridded in rows of five, and I was on the 9th row! This is where my motocross background came in handy. In motocross, you all start from the same line. You could be 40 abreast! And only three or four of you are going to fit into the first turn. Getting a good start is crucial. When the green flag dropped at Summit Point, I passed everyone on the three rows ahead of me before they even started moving! As the race progressed (12 laps), some of them with better roadrace skills than me caught me back up, but I ended up in the top 20, in no danger of winning anything, but I had a lot of fun.

I ran a couple more races that summer and learned some tricks with the bike. For instance, you could remove the air cleaner element for racing and pick up a little bit of power. You could also cut the exhaust baffles to about half their normal length and pick up a little more power (not strictly legal!). There are oversize pistons available that are intended for the repair of worn out cylinders. If you get the biggest ones and bore the cylinders to fit, you pick up about 10cc of engine displacement and it is still considered to be stock. There was also a rule about the instruments (speedometer and tachometer) that they had to be in place unless they were broken in a crash that weekend. You really want the tachometer, but the speedometer just adds weight, and if it is gone, you can tuck in a little bit lower and still see through the space where it was. So, the trick was to have the speedometer in place for tech inspection, but "accidentally" drop the bike afterwards and have it break!

Racing season is now over, but I am jazzed for motorsports, and I decide to go to the United States Grand Prix at Watkins Glen, NY (near Corning), which was held in early October. This was for Formula 1 cars, and it was the last race of a season that had Niki Lauda (Ferrari) and Emerson Fittipaldi (McLaren) fighting it out for the driver's world championship. My plan was to go to bed early on Saturday night, then get up about midnight and ride my RD350 to Watkins Glen, watch the race, then ride home in time to get some sleep before going to work on Monday morning. I had a backpack to carry 2-stroke oil, some water, and a sandwich, and I had enough money for gas and my admission to the track. I had a wool turtleneck sweater to wear underneath my leather jacket to keep me warm. Midnight came, and off I went. Well, that sweater did a pretty good job when standing still. At 70 MPH in cold, damp autumn air... not so good! It was about a nine-hour drive to the track, and I was pretty damn cold when I got there. Also, all those modifications that I made for racing turned out to be not so comfortable on a nine-hour ride. And, when racing, you are not allowed to have a side stand on the bike. It didn't occur to me that one might be handy when I got where I was going! I had to find something to lean the bike against whenever I stopped. I got pulled over by a cop around Binghamton, NY. I was probably speeding, but not by much. I think he looked at me and assumed that I had drugs in my backpack. As he walked up to me, I noticed that the wire from the front brake light switch had become disconnected (a common problem with RD350s), and I discretely plugged it back in. Sure enough, the cop asked me if I knew my brake light was out. I said no, and applied the front brake...

"Looks fine to me," I said.

He scratched his head and said, "So you must have been downshifting to slow down?"

"That's right, officer," I said.

He inspected the contents of my backpack, counseled me to watch my speed, and went on his way. I must have said "Yes, sir," about 20 times.

I get to the track about 10:00 AM and find a fence to lean my bike against. The sun is coming out, and I can finally get a little warmth into my frozen bones. I didn't have a grandstand seat, just general admission, but amazingly, in those days, that allowed you into the pits! I wandered my way around the track and watched the race from several vantage points. It was a good race with Lauda leading and Fittipaldi close behind, but with Niki's teammate, Clay Regazzoni in between them. Regazzoni managed to get his car sideways in every turn, blocking Fittipaldi from making up time on Lauda. This would all be quite illegal these days, but back then all Fittipaldi could do was to wave his fist and curse. Lauda won and clinched his first world championship.

Back on my RD350…another little thing about race bikes, they don't have kick starters (they could flop outwards in a turn and cause an accident). You start the bike by putting the transmission into 2nd gear, pull in the clutch and push the bike, then hop your butt onto the seat and let the clutch out. If the bike is running well, the rear wheel turns the engine over, and it starts right up. You swing your leg over the seat and ride away. However, you need some space in which to do this. Also, it doesn't work near as well on a dirt surface, because the rear wheel just locks up when you let the clutch out. I managed to get it started on the second try in the crowded dirt parking lot. Traffic crawled through Corning, but I finally got on my way home, freezing again. I got home around 2:00 AM and got into work about 8:30 feeling pretty worn out. The next year, I hitch-hiked to the Grand Prix!

The next racing season, I branched out from Summit Point and went with some buddies to Charlotte Motor Speedway. It rained, and it turned out that I was better at riding in the rain than some of my competitors, probably due to the motocross background and being used to slipping and sliding. I managed to make it into the top

10 for the first time. And I raced against this new 14 year-old kid named Freddy Spencer. He won!

That summer, I was riding to work and stopped at the nearby 7-11 for a cup of coffee. There was a service road that paralleled the main road, and I was on the service road when a car blazed in from the main road right in front of me. I hit his left front fender and landed on the hood of the car, with my coffee in a bag in my right hand…it just slipped out of my grasp and fell on the ground, spilling all the coffee. A 16-year-old kid was driving the car, and he was absolutely terrified. I told him what he needed to do: call your father, give me the insurance information, and buy me another damn cup of coffee! I was close enough to walk to the shop and get the shop truck to pick up my bike. We got the insurance adjuster to the shop that day and got an approval for the repair estimate, which included replacing the bent front forks! Check in hand, I thought I could find better ways to spend it, and I straightened the front forks again! Back on the road that night.

I was starting to get the hang of roadracing and began to collect some trophies. Some friends from Maryland asked me to ride with them in the WERA (ERA morphed into WERA as they added West coast races) Endurance Racing series. The bike was, of course, a Yamaha RD350. I helped prep the bike for racing and we had some successes. The centerpiece of the series was the 30 Hours of Rockingham. We contested it with five riders, with me getting most of the nighttime duties. Except for the pit area, the track was not really lit, and the RD350's headlight was pretty anemic. I would follow other bikes that had much better lighting systems, then pass them only to find that I couldn't see! The next strategy was to wait for a faster bike with good lights to pass us both, then tuck in behind him for as long as I could. Around 2:00 AM, fog rolled in, and I could hardly see at all. I had to ride with my face shield open in order to see anything, but I kept at it and just racked up as many laps as I could. In the morning, one of our riders crashed and limped back to the pits with bent handlebars and a broken front brake lever. One of us scrounged around the pits to find a replacement lever…not a problem, it's an RD350! In the meantime, I did my best to straighten the bent handlebars with partial success. Then I went out on the bike to shake it down. I found it had a horrible wobble going around the banking, until I figured out that I was trying to hold the handlebars straight ahead, and they weren't straight. So, I relaxed and let the bike find its own line, and then held the bars where they ended up. Wobble gone! Feels a little weird, but it works and we are back out racing. At 4:00 PM, the race is over, and we have 2nd place in the 400cc Production Class! We are thoroughly whupped, and the poor bike looks like it has been through a war, but it ran great all day and all night.

We gave the bike some TLC and entered it in several more of the WERA Endurance series, coming in 2nd in class for the season.

In the meantime, I was working at a Kawasaki/Suzuki shop near Fredericksburg, VA. It was kind of a long way away, but I made good money there and liked the people. I rode my RD back and forth to save on gas money. At work, I would lean it against the dumpster (still no sidestand). One day, a guy poked his nose into the shop and asked if that bike was being thrown out, because he would take it for nothing if it was!

No, it's not being thrown out.

I took it out to Summit Point again that summer for a WERA event. In a heat race on Saturday, I was trying to pass a whole group of slower riders in the S-Turns…the maneuver didn't quite work, and I had to run off the track into the grass. Shouldn't be a big problem for a former motocrosser. You stand up on the foot pegs and get your weight back a little, so the front wheel can glide over the bumps. What I didn't realize was that there was a drainage ditch, hidden by the grass. I hit it hard and got slammed down on my left side. I dislocated my left shoulder and sprained my left ankle. They took me off to the local hospital, where they put on ACE bandages, gave me something for pain, gave me one crutch and sent me back to the track. My buddies helped me get the bike into my pick-up truck. I hobbled around and drank enough beer that I managed to sleep in the truck. After Sunday's races, a friend drove my truck back home for me, and I took a couple days off work to recuperate. By Wednesday, I was feeling good enough to drive into work. There, my buddies helped me get the bike off the truck and into my work bay. The impact had been directly on the front wheel, and, of course, the front forks were bent…again! One more time on the press…it is getting harder to get them really straight, but I manage to get them to be fully functional, if not pretty. I replaced the front rim this time, as it had been bashed and straightened a few times already. My bike was fully healed before I was!

My confidence at racing was increasing, and I began to have higher aspirations than production class club racing, so I bought a very nice, used Yamaha TZ250 race bike. It was a couple of years old, but it was beautiful and had been very well prepared.

> *NOTE: A Yamaha TZ250 was a pure racing bike and ran in what was known as Grand Prix (GP) class. In the day, if you had aspirations to be a professional, you needed to be fast on a 250. Incidentally, while it was designed from the beginning to be a pure racing bike, the engine cases came directly from a Yamaha RD250! But the cylinders were water-cooled, it had a dry clutch, a fairing to tuck in behind and ran slick racing tires. It weighed about 100 lbs less than an RD250 did and made about twice the horsepower.*

I campaigned it in WERA that year with some success and finished #3 nationally. So, I began to plan for greater things next year, starting with Daytona! Daytona Speed Week always took place around the end of February/beginning of March and was the first big motorcycle race of the season. The top Grand Prix racers from Europe would come over to contest it just to shake down their new race bikes, and it was the centerpiece of the American Motorcyclist Association's (AMA) professional racing series. I applied for my professional license and was granted a Novice Pro Roadrace license. Preparations for the race involved getting to Daytona and finding accommodations on my pretty limited budget. A good friend hooked me up with a girl named Joan, who was also a racer (she had ridden with us at Rockingham), who wanted to go to Daytona, and had plans to stay in a campground. She had all the gear, and we shared expenses, so it worked out well. I had borrowed a motorcycle trailer that had room for three bikes, so we towed my race bike and her street bike behind my Volkswagen Scirocco. Her street bike was, of course, an RD350! It was tricked out with a fairing and looked much cooler than stock, but underneath, it was a good old Yamaha. She could then get around while I was at the track practicing for my race. At one point, her battery went dead, and I diagnosed a shorted rectifier. Off to the local Yamaha store, an easy part to replace and she was back in business.

I was quickly realizing that my three-year-old TZ250 was horribly slow compared to the guys who had brand new ones. The fast guys would reach 150 MPH on the banking...I managed 145 at my fastest. That might sound fast, but when somebody who you passed in the infield blows right by you on the banking, it feels dog slow! However, being a professional rider in the pits at Daytona was incredibly cool. All of my idols were there: Kenny Roberts, Eddie Lawson, and the now-famous Freddie Spencer. My picture was in the program, and a little kid who sounded Dutch asked me for my autograph on his program. Did I feel cool or what?

There were about 150 guys vying for 80 starting spots in my race, so they broke us into two groups for qualifying, with me gridded at the back of my group. I got my usual good start, but leaning into turn one, the handlebar of the guy next to me caught on my leathers and held me up for a few seconds, long enough to lose touch with the leaders. In the end I qualified 82nd, classified as 2nd alternate. My instructions were to be in the pits, ready to race in case two other bikes ahead of me fail to make it to the grid. That is what happened, and I started the race in 80th place. A long, hard race later, I ended up 40th. Not making anyone's news report, but it didn't feel too bad.

Back to reality, Joan and I started going together, and I drove us to some WERA races. She had met this young man who was interested in taking up roadracing, and she sort of took him on as a protegé. He had a street bike that was nice but would not have been competitive in any of the available classes, so he needed a race bike. Hmmm, my poor old, thoroughly thrashed RD350 was sitting in my garage, feeling neglected. I sold it to him for $350. There was a WERA race coming up at Summit Point, so Joan and I went there and helped him get registered, go through tech inspection, run practice etc. On Sunday, he took 3rd place and got a trophy in his very first race…on my old, clapped out RD350!…that had had the front forks bent and straightened three times!

By this time, Yamaha had superseded the RD350 with a more modern RD400, that had more torque, but not more horsepower, and it was heavier and had a more plush ride quality. Good things for riding on the street, but not for racing!

As more and more emissions rules came into play, 2-stroke street motorcycles were phased out, and, in the early 1980s racing series began to reflect this trend, with classes based around 4-cylinder 4-stroke street engines. Yamaha's last hurrah for the 2-stroke street bike was a Kenny Roberts replica (Yellow & Black paint scheme) that had catalytic converters in order to meet emissions requirements. That made it pretty expensive, and very few were sold.

There are still some of us who remember the good qualities of 2-stroke bikes, and of RD350s in particular.

Mecum Auctions/mecum.com

1974 RD350 in stock condition

Note the footpeg bracket that wraps underneath the exhaust pipe. This is the first thing that drags on the ground in a turn. If you remove this bracket and make foot peg mounts using the buddy-peg mount to the rear, you can greatly increase the potential lean angle of the bike.

Also note the front brake caliper (black with circular silver center). This was a great feature of Yamahas of the day. It is a dual-action caliper (presses from both sides), and it was steel, which is heavy, but did not flex at all. This means that you could use it hard and repeatedly without any brake fade…a big advantage on certain race tracks where other bikes would lose braking efficiency in the course of a race.

SLOT CAR RACING

L ife at a motorcycle shop in the winter can be pretty dull. Especially as a mechanic.

You can paint the shop…that only takes a day or so. Maybe the shop truck needs maintenance. The Sales Department may have taken in some clunkers on trade in order to close a deal. Fixing those up to make them saleable takes a little time, especially since you're expected to do it with minimal cost in parts. When things get really slow, you can sharpen a chainsaw chain and make $2.00! (Hey, that bought a six-pack of Budweiser in those days).

We made good money in the spring and summer, especially July, which was crash-job month. It was pretty predictable. People would buy new bikes in the spring and start crashing them in June as the weather got nice. We had the added advantage of being a Kawasaki shop near a Marine base. The young Marines would buy the Kawasaki 500 (a 3-cylinder 2-stroke) that was reasonably priced, really fast, and had some very evil handling characteristics. When they crashed and it was being repaired by insurance, they always wanted us to make them faster. I guess it didn't hurt enough the first time they crashed…they were Marines, after all.

Most of us at the shop raced motorcycles on the weekends. Randy and Jay had professional motocross licenses. I did roadracing at Summit Point, W. VA; Stu rode enduros and hare scrambles. Bannister, the sales manager, also rode motocross, but not at the professional level, and he always rode a Kawasaki (he WAS sales manager at a Kawasaki shop), which was a disadvantage in motocross at the time.

Monday mornings would be about how each of us did at our races over the weekend. Sometimes you didn't need to ask…bent motorcycle and an arm in a cast…guess it didn't go so well! And after work during the week, we would be working on our race bikes and shooting the shit with each other. Beer came out at 5:00 PM sharp. The problem was that the service manager, Stu, was British, and it didn't occur to him to put the beer into the refrigerator!

Then comes winter. There's no racing.

The old shop had a loft where the Parts Department kept salvaged bikes, old engines, and any stuff that might be useful at some point. They had set up a makeshift table with saw horses and some plywood. One day we noticed a box that had slot car track in it. We got it out and started laying it out on the table. It turned out that we had enough track to make a really long, four-lane slot car track. It was G-Scale track, and Gary, from Parts, had a couple of G-Scale slot cars, so we tried it out that evening.

I had a hand in the track design, and I started with the Mulsanne Straight, named after the seven-mile straight at Le Mans. It ran the maximum length of the table, and like the Mulsanne, there was a hairpin turn at the end. Ten more tight turns brought you back around to the Mulsanne Straight again. When we tried the track out with Gary's two cars that evening and we found out two fun things:

Our group was incredibly competitive and would try desperately to win at whatever type of racing we could find.

If you went flat out down the Mulsanne Straight and didn't back off in time to make the hairpin turn, the car would fly off into the air, out of the loft, and land down in the shop below, somewhat the worse for wear.

The little cars accelerated really quickly, and could get into big trouble if you were too aggressive. Finesse with the controller was all-important.

The next day all of us mechanics went off to the local hobby shop and bought our own G-scale slot cars and controllers for some intense competition that evening. That's when it began to get interesting...

I started by taking the body off the chassis of my car (a Formula 1 car replica). I discovered that the car was a lot faster without the body and tried racing it that way. Immediately a rule was established that you needed to have the body on the car. For one thing, you couldn't tell the cars apart without the body on. So I got out my Dremel tool and started grinding every bit of unnecessary plastic off the underside of the body. There were four attachment points, and they were the only places where any strength was needed. I cut the weight in half, and the car was clearly faster. The other guys, of course, started grinding on their cars as well.

Randy was frustrated with his car's acceleration and had the idea of taking the controller apart and checking out the rheostat. Sure enough, his was not going the full length of the resistor, so his car never got full power. He fixed that, not without everyone else noticing...My controller was sticky, which made it hard to control the speed of the car, so it had to come apart and get cleaned and lubricated. I also tweaked it to give me a little more peak power. This made the car a lot easier to drive.

The cars had these little gumball tires that came in various degrees of stickiness. Back we went to the hobby shop to get the stickiest ones. The tires were just stretched over the wheels, and with the sticky ones, you could get the wheels to spin inside the tires under acceleration, so we had to glue the tires onto the wheels. Bannister went a step further and tried applying turntable belt dressing to the tires. It made them incredibly sticky and worked really well, but the dressing was actually melting the plastic track surface, so we made him stop using it (another new rule!).

One day, I had my car apart and was fanatically looking for ways to make it faster. I looked at the brushes that contacted the electrodes on the track, and decided that they might work better if I coated them with silver solder. It worked, but it wore off, so you needed to do it every day. I also messed with their spring tension .more tension equaled better electrical contact, but also more drag. Lots of testing was needed to optimize this parameter.

Jay thought he could improve performance by modifying the pin in the front of the car that engaged the slot in the track (thus the name: "slot cars"). Less depth meant less drag, but it also meant that the car tended to fly off the track more easily in the turns. Again, lots of testing time to optimize it.

We now had seven or eight guys vying for four spots on the starting grid each evening (not everyone was there each time), so we needed to have heat races, with two cars advancing to the final from each heat. We also discovered that we had a starting problem. When the starter (usually Gary) would say, "Ready, Set, Go," Randy and Jay (the pro motocross guys) would always go on "Set." They denied any wrongdoing until I privately told Gary to start a race with "Ready, Set," and to never say "Go." Sure enough, Randy and Jay were half-way around the lap before they realized that he hadn't said "Go!" The other cars were still sitting on the starting line.

We came up with a solution where Gary held the power plug unplugged, so there was no power to the transformer until he said "Go." Everybody just held their controllers flat out, and we finally got clean, fair starts!

Whoever won for the evening got the honor of buying beer for the next event…and that was okay because it was an honor!

Eventually spring came, and real work and real racing started to supersede our slot car time. By the next winter, the old shop was torn down, and we moved to a nice new facility that had no place for a slot car track. That shop closed the next winter, and we all went on to our different fames and fortunes, none of which involved slot cars. But it was fun while it lasted!

www.ingramcontent.com/pod-product-compliance
Lightning Source LLC
Chambersburg PA
CBHW060342130626
46553CB00003B/1086